Dumfries and Galloway

40 Coast & Country Walks

The author and publisher have made every effort to ensure that the information in this publication is accurate, and accept no responsibility whatsoever for any loss, injury or inconvenience experienced by any person or persons whilst using this book.

published by
pocket mountains ltd
Holm Street, Moffat,
Dumfries and Galloway DG109EB
pocketmountains.com

ISBN: 978-1-9070250-3-7

Text copyright © J Fallis

Photography copyright © Allan Devlin (www.sw-images-scotland.co.uk)

The right of J Fallis to be identified as the Author of this work has been asserted by him in accordance with the Copyright, Designs and Patents Act 1988

A catalogue record for this book is available from the British Library

All route maps are based on 1945 Popular Edition Ordnance Survey material and revised from field surveys by Pocket Mountains Ltd. © Pocket Mountains Ltd.

Printed in Poland

Introduction

Dumfries and Galloway inhabits the southwest corner of Scotland and offers all that is expected of Scotland – wide rivers, deep forests, rolling hills and a glorious coastline, along with an unexpectedly mild climate. In addition, it provides space and solitude in abundance. Covering an area of almost 4000 sq km, it is the third largest county in Scotland but with a population of less than 150,000.

South and west lies a 300km coastline of sandy beaches, mudflats, natural harbours and spectacular cliffs. It is a haven for wildlife, particularly migratory birds, as indicated by the number of RSPB reserves. Loch Ken is the site of a successful red kite reintroduction programme, and ospreys have raised young in several locations locally. With 97 Sites of Special Scientific Interest (SSSI) in the county, it is home to around 20 percent of the country's red squirrel population and is the only location in Scotland where the natterjack toad can be found.

In geography, Dumfries and Galloway is unexpectedly diverse. With the coast never far from any point, the west has a strong maritime flavour. Inland and eastwards lies a belt of fertile farmland with low rolling hills, closest in appearance to the landscape of Northern Ireland. This gives way to moorland, forest and mountain terrain. Draining north to south are major rivers – the Luce, Cree, Fleet, Ken/Dee, Urr, Nith, Annan and Esk – historically key in shaping the development of settlements and transport routes while now providing ample opportunities for recreation, conservation and energy creation.

The county is home to the Galloway Forest Park – 482 sq km of forest, moor and mountain. It boasts the highest peak in Southern Scotland, the Merrick, at 843m. The Southern Upland Way meanders across Dumfries and Galloway for part of its 340km course, starting in Portpatrick and ending in Cockburnspath. Throughout the area, the hillwalking is superb and there is rarely an issue with parking or crowded summits!

Dumfries and Galloway is a modern designation for the old counties of Galloway and Dumfriesshire. Historically, Galloway consisted of Wigtownshire (West Galloway) and the Stewartry (East Galloway) with Dumfriesshire to their east. Wigtownshire is subdivided into the Rhins, the far west around Stranraer, and the Machars, the low-lying peninsula south of Newton Stewart. Eastwards, the Stewartry of Kirkcudbrightshire extends from Kirkcudbright in the south to the Glenkens in the north. Dumfriesshire consist of three river valleys – the Nith, Annan and Esk – and has only 34km of coastline, giving it a much more landward attitude than Galloway. Being located close to the English border, the valleys have been major thoroughfares for visitors through the centuries, some of whom have been of a less than friendly persuasion.

This book is divided into five chapters, in turn covering the Rhins; the rest of the old county of Wigtownshire from the Galloway

Forest Park to the Machars; the remote hill country of the Glenkens to Gatehouse; Castle Douglas and the coast to the River Urr catchment; and finally around Dumfries and Nithsdale.

These 40 walks include some of the best routes along the coast, over moor and mountain, across farmland and through some of the more picturesque towns, villages and conservation areas. Although there are many good forestry walks in Dumfries and Galloway, most have been excluded due both to their extensive coverage elsewhere and in order to give prominence to some great but less-known routes: visit *forestry.gov.uk* for more details on forest walks. With stronger cultural and geographical associations with the Borders region, Eskdale and most of Annandale are also omitted from this guide.

History

The area has always been a crossroads for visitors, due both to the extensive coastline and the easily navigated river valleys of Dumfriesshire. It is littered with prehistoric monuments and relics, while there is plenty of evidence of Roman activity. Christianity in Scotland began in Galloway with the earliest known Christian memorials and the various dedications to St Ninian who settled at Whithorn. Before the Reformation, pilgrims from all corners of Scotland descended on the shrine of St Ninian in Whithorn – among them Robert the Bruce and Mary Queen of Scots. These pilgrimage routes helped settlements such as Dalry, Creetown, Newton Stewart and

the Isle of Whithorn to develop.

The Middle Ages was a time of great upheaval, indicated by the number of mottes, castles and towerhouses built here then. Galloway displayed a spectacularly independent outlook and was only incorporated into Scotland after invasion by Alexander III in 1234. This contrasted with Dumfriesshire – and Annandale, in particular. The Wars of Independence were partly attributed to competing claims to the Scottish crown from the Lord of Galloway, John Balliol, and the Lord of Annan, Robert Bruce and later his grandson Robert the Bruce. For Annandale and Nithsdale, conflict was endemic as it sat on the western edge of the England-Scotland border. Before the Union of 1603, this area was a hotbed of family feuds, cattle thieving and border raids or reiving.

The Reformation stopped pilgrimages to Whithorn, but gave birth to another religious movement – the Covenanters. This presbyterian Christian group signed a covenant against royal changes to worship. In the English Civil War, a Covenanting army fought with parliament, forcing Charles I to surrender. But when, with the Restoration of Charles II, they became a persecuted minority, their most stubborn adherents clung to the southwest of Scotland. Many of the walks in this guide pass monuments and graves to 'martyred' Covenanters killed by government forces.

After the Union of the Crowns in 1603, the area began to develop as a major transport route to Ireland for trade and for moving soldiers and families to and from the plantations of Ulster. Following the Act of Union in 1707, the region prospered further due to agricultural reforms which cleared the land of people and enclosed fields. The reforms led to waves of emigration to North America and Australia/New Zealand via ports such as Kirkcudbright and Wigtown, as well as establishing drove routes to England for cattle and sheep.

The Jacobite rebellions, of 1715 and 1745 passed through Dumfriesshire but gained little support from locals, partly due to the area's strong Calvinist background. The fortunes brought about by legitimate trade with Ireland were supplemented by prolific smuggling, assisted by the many small harbours, tidal rivers and coves.

Though a rural idyll today, the region did not escape industrialisation. Wanlockhead has been mined for precious metals since Roman times while Gatehouse of Fleet, Castle Douglas and Newton Stewart developed unsuccessful cotton and woollen milling industries. Allied to the industry came improved transport links, such as the Telford bridge near Kirkcudbright and the magnificent 20-arch railway viaduct near Gatehouse of Fleet.

Today, Dumfries and Galloway is best known for agriculture, forestry, wildlife and tourism, but it has a strong artistic tradition. Its most famous former resident is Robert Burns, who lived in and around Dumfries between 1788 and 1796. Kirkcudbright has long been a mecca for artists, most famously the Glasgow Boys, while many locations in Galloway were used in the 1973 film *The Wicker Man*.

Safety and transport

Many of the routes in this volume are waymarked and suitable for families, with a good number that are buggy-friendly. Although Dumfries and Galloway is known for its mild climate, some of these walks are on high ground and many are by the coast, where weather conditions can change quickly. It is recommended that stout shoes or walking boots are worn and appropriate clothing carried on all routes. Sketch maps in this book are intended only as an aid to navigation: for all routes on open ground or in remote country, walkers should take the relevant Harvey/OS map and compass – and know how to use them.

Access

The Land Reform Act (Scotland) of 2003 gave walkers the right of access over most of Scotland's countryside, but this right brings responsibilities. Much of Dumfries and Galloway is a working landscape and many of these walks enter areas of conservation or scientific interest, so refer to the Scottish Outdoor Access Code if in doubt and please remember to control dogs during lambing season; be aware, too, that seasonal shooting is a major local business in some parts of the region.

Where possible, walks have been devised with public transport access in mind, but this is no easy task in an area with such limited public transport options. Even in areas where there are bus services, timings may not fit the walks, so advance planning is essential. For more information, visit **www.swestrans.org.uk**

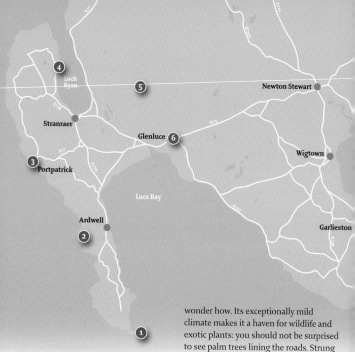

The evocative Rhins of Galloway, the name given to the most southwesterly corner of Scotland, is thought to have come from the Gaelic *Na Rannaibh*, 'the point' or 'headland'. The peninsula which makes up the Rhins of Galloway runs for 32km from north to south, instantly identifiable on maps by its distinct hammer shape. Stranraer is the main settlement to the east, the Rhins to the west of the town defined by an almost island feel.

This is a tranquil place with an unspoilt landscape and a feeling of having been passed by, though its beauty will make you wonder how. Its exceptionally mild climate makes it a haven for wildlife and exotic plants: you should not be surprised to see palm trees lining the roads. Strung out along the 'headland' are the three main settlements of Leswalt, Portpatrick and Drummore, with other scattered villages never far from the sea.

The eastern boundary of the Rhins is a matter of some debate, but the routes in this chapter offer the broadest possible interpretation, stretching east of Stranraer to the valley of the River Luce, where the landscape is characterised by rolling farmland and moors. The key settlements over here are New Luce and Glenluce. All of the routes in this chapter are accessible from Stranraer.

On Killantringan beach near Portpatrick ▶

Rhins of Galloway

Mull of Galloway

Distance 3.5km **Time** 1 hour + allow time for detour to Lagvag and visitor centre **Terrain** tarmac roads and muddy fields; exposed clifftop paths unsuitable in windy weather – use inland alternative **Map** OS Landranger 82 **Access** start from the public car park next to the RSPB Reserve wall; drivers, take the A716 to Drummore, then follow the signposts

Visit the windswept peninsula of Scotland's most southerly point, with a rich history and great views of cliffs teeming with seabirds. The café, lighthouse and RSPB visitor centre are open seasonally: check before visiting.

From the car park, walk back along the road for about 700m to reach two lonely wooden posts on your left, with a cairn visible on the high ground behind. Turn off the road to head up to this. Known as Kennedy's Cairn, its history is vague but it offers great views around the Mull and can be climbed using stone steps set into the side. The walk provides views in all directions and, on a good day, the Lake District, Machars, Isle of Man and Ireland are all visible.

From the cairn, continue across the field towards the cliffs and a gate in the fence. Here, you can either go through the gate and follow the path along the cliff edge or stay on the inland side of the fence and head down to the earthworks. The inland option gives a good alternative in windy weather and for those less confident

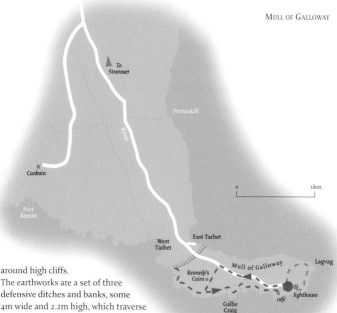

To
Stranraer

Portankill

Cardrain

Port
Kemin

0   1km

West   East Tarbet
Tarbet   Mull of Galloway   Lagvag
        Kennedy's
        Cairn   lighthouse
                                          café
        Gallie
        Craig

around high cliffs.

The earthworks are a set of three defensive ditches and banks, some 4m wide and 2.2m high, which traverse the Mull for 400m and are thought to be from the 1st century BC. Simply return to the car park using the path or the road. From the clifftop path, a gate immediately below the café gives access back to the car park.

If you have made the effort to get to the Mull, you won't want to miss out on the reserve itself, which is at its finest in late spring. From the car park, follow the markers to the visitor centre and then on to Lagvag Point. This gives great views of the seabirds that nest on the cliffs and in the grass and heather around the reserve. These include guillemots, kittiwakes, fulmars and razorbills, while linnets can be found in the heather and grassland

around Lagvag. Keep a sharp eye on the waters for the occasional basking shark.

On the way here, you'll also find the most photographed feature of the Mull – the lighthouse. Engineered by Robert Stevenson and built by the Northern Lighthouse Board in 1828, it stands 26m high and there are 114 steps to the top (fee to enter). The original five-ton lens was lit by paraffin and took two minutes 45 seconds to revolve, but the site is now electrified and has been unmanned since 1971. The original cottage for the keeper and his family is now a holiday home.

◀ The lighthouse

Ardwell Bay and Doon Broch

Distance 3km Time 1 hour
Terrain **sandy beach and grassy tracks**
Map **OS Landranger 83** Access **turn off the A716 at Lake Cottage (between Sandhead and Ardwell), go straight through the crossroads at Clachanmore and continue for 3km; the road is narrow and rutted beyond West/High Ardwell**

Pack a picnic and enjoy a secluded sandy bay that offers solitude, rockpools and a remarkable piece of ancient history.

The beach at Ardwell Bay is a good site for wildlife watching, with wading birds found searching for food and grey seals sometimes spotted around the bay. This is an exceptionally pretty short walk of two parts. From the car park, head down to the beach and turn right to stroll along the sand until it ends, continuing on an obvious path along the grassy area behind the rocks. The building at the far end of the beach is called Salt Pans, alluding to the area's proliferation of salt-panning sites which produced small volumes of salt for food preservation. Before refrigeration, salt was a valuable commodity and, as a result of the mild climate, it was fairly easy to produce it locally by capturing seawater in shallow pans which was then drawn out by natural evaporation. There were two pans in the immediate vicinity.

Depending on the tide and time, you can walk along this path to a convenient point and simply return to the sandy beach, an obvious turning place being at the end of the grassy area where the route continues across the rocky coastline.

Back at the beach, head to the other end

◀ Cottages at Ardwell

and cross the stile into a field.
Skirt around the edge of the
field and follow the path as
it meanders up ground
that is slowly slipping
into the sea. The path
crosses an old wire fence
and is waymarked. From
this point, look out for
a low promontory
with what looks like
a pile of stones
located towards
the end. This
is, in fact, the
ruins of
Doon Broch:
on closer
inspection,
you can
make out
the outline
of the
building. The
broch is one of only
a handful found outwith Northern
Scotland – with two entrances, one facing
the sea and one the land. It is believed to
have been built between 100BC and
200AD. From here, simply retrace your
steps to the beach.

A nearby point of interest is the
Kirkmadrine Stones, the oldest Scottish
Christian monuments outside Whithorn.
They date from the 5th century and bear
Latin inscriptions, representing an early
Christian cemetery of some importance,
possibly an offshoot of the Whithorn
settlement. The stones can be found in
the porch of Kirkmadrine Church, which
you'll see signposted on the way to the
walk. East of Ardwell Bay, reached via the
Clachanmore crossroads, you'll also find
the lovely Ardwell House: the gardens,
though not the 18th-century house, are
open to the public in summer (fee).

Portpatrick coast and glen

Distance 5km **Time** 1 hour 30
Map OS Landranger 83 **Terrain** tarmac,
paths and tracks NB access to Dunskey
Glen may be restricted during shooting
season (mid-Oct to mid-Feb); a tour of
Port Mora and Port Kale makes a lovely
alternative at such times **Access** bus (367,
411) from Stranraer

**A circular walk from a beautiful town,
along clifftops and through the peaceful
woodland of Dunskey Glen with superb
views and wildlife at every turn.**

Today Portpatrick is a picturesque port,
but throughout its history it was the
gateway to Scotland from Ireland. It really
developed during the first half of the 17th
century when the Lord of Dunskey
obtained a royal warrant to make
Portpatrick the main port for travel
between Scotland and the plantations in
Ulster. Between 1662 and 1848, this town

was the principal point of entry for cattle,
troops shipping to Ireland, mail and
passenger ferries and, for many years,
Portpatrick for the Irish was the same as
Gretna for the English, a location for
hurried marriages. However, the exposed
nature of the port meant business
gradually moved to Stranraer.

From the car park at the harbour, walk
towards the coastguard building and
public toilets, then turn right and find the
information board at the start of the
Southern Upland Way (SUW). Climb the
steps, carved with a series of geology
facts, that mark the start of the 340km
long-distance trail. As the path meanders
up and along the cliffs, it passes some radio
masts to the right, before turning right to
join a tarmac path between the cliffs and
the golf course. This begins to descend to
Port Mora, passing a delightful waterfall
on the way to the pebbly bay. Cross to the

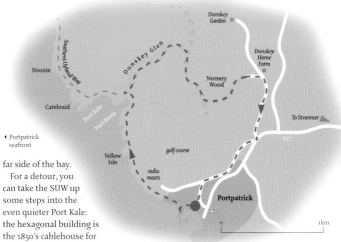

◄ Portpatrick
seafront

far side of the bay.

For a detour, you can take the SUW up some steps into the even quieter Port Kale: the hexagonal building is the 1850's cablehouse for telegram connections to Ireland. Otherwise, follow a rising grassy path into Dunskey Glen to meet a dirt estate track, turning right here to pass a house. During commercial shooting season, walkers are requested to phone ahead (details at www.dunskey.com), and at all times to keep to the waymarked routes. The track plunges into a lovely wood and then winds uphill with the burn below left. At a T-junction (red metal gate and white signposts), turn right along the edge of the woodland with increasingly good views across the golf course towards Portpatrick.

After crossing a burn, you branch left at a Y-junction (signposted to the tearoom) and continue to a T-junction opposite Dunskey Home Farm, where there is an honesty box for use of the glen. Turn right here. If you wish to detour to the lovely Dunskey Garden with its walled and woodland gardens, maze, glass-houses, tearoom and gift shop (seasonal opening; fee), there is a turn-off on the left just past the farm. Otherwise, shortly after the turn-off, the track reaches another Y-junction, where you turn right to pass a group of houses and Sawmill Cottage. A downhill stretch now follows, with great views out to sea along the way. Where the track crosses a burn and meets the A77, turn right and follow the road to the war memorial before making another right turn onto Heugh Road.

Follow this road towards the golf club to meet Braefield Road, then turn left to take this downhill. After around 100m, steps on the right drop you down to a road, where you keep right to walk along Welsh Place to the car park.

13

Wig Bay round

Distance 3.5km **Time** 1 hour
Terrain roads, sand and muddy tracks
NB during exceptional high tides, the bay
may become impassable
Map OS Landranger 83 **Access** bus (408)
from Stranraer to Kirkcolm

**A gentle walk around a small bay that is a
haven for migratory birds. Watch ferries
pass and look out for wartime relics.**

The village and farming community of
Kirkcolm is located in the Northern Rhins
with water on three sides. As you would
expect, fishing has been one source of
income here, but it was also once a centre
of home-produced muslin embroidery.
From Kirkcolm, it is possible to continue
north by road to the northern tip of the
Rhins for views out over the Atlantic.

Start from the car park at the end of Wig
Bay, located just at the point where the
road leaves the coastline, around 1km
south of Kirkcolm. (It is possible to start
the walk from the end of Fishers Road in
Kirkcolm, where there is limited parking.)
Follow the track towards the end of the
bay: it begins as tarmac but eventually
becomes gravel. Care should be taken as
vehicles do use the track. This stage of the
route gives excellent views across Loch
Ryan to Stranraer and you will also find a
wealth of birdlife in the bay, with many
breeds of ducks, gulls and waders present.
The sandbank of The Scar is especially
significant for the number of terns that
nest on the shingle in summer. You will

find interpretation boards provided at several intervals along the route.

At the WWII observation post, turn left and walk along the back of the beach for around 800m until a set of signs and information boards signal a left turn to go inland. This leg gives you the chance to see Ailsa Craig out beyond Loch Ryan. Ailsa Craig is a remnant of an extinct volcano, a granite plug that stands 338m high. Its main claim to fame is that all curling stones are quarried from its unique type of granite. (For a closer look at a curling stone, visit the visitor centre at Bladnoch Distillery.)

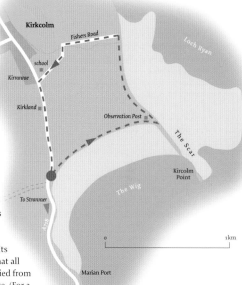

After crossing a wooden footbridge, the path takes you to the end of Fishers Road. In summer, the fields to the left are often filled with skylarks and finches feeding and singing. The road leads to a T-junction, where you turn left to return to the start: there is a pavement most of the way. Keep a look-out for remnants of WWII on both sides of the road. During the war, Wig Bay was a major maintenance and refitting base for seaplanes – at its peak, more than 170 flying boats and 1000 RAF personnel were based in and around the bay. Loch Ryan was a vital port in both world wars for convoy shipping travelling across the North Atlantic and, in the Second World War, Cairnryan (directly across the water) was prepared as an emergency port should the Mersey and Clyde ports have been put out of action. At the end of the war, the German U-boat fleets were surrendered and transported to Cairnryan before being scuttled in the Atlantic.

New Luce and the Caves of Kilhern

Distance 9km **Time** 2 hours 30
Terrain roads and muddy tracks;
relatively long but gradual ascent
Map OS Landranger 82 **Access** bus (410)
from Stranraer to New Luce

This is a wonderful walk along quiet lanes and across moorland to visit a Neolithic burial site and get a taste of the Southern Upland Way. The route starts and finishes in the pretty village of New Luce.

A picturesque village built on the junction of five roads and two rivers (the Main Water and Cross Water of Luce), New Luce gets its name as a result of a parish boundary change in 1628. From the village hall, walk back along the quiet road towards Glenluce. The road has some sharp bends so care should be taken. After around 2km, turn left and go through the gate onto a farm track that is signposted

for the Southern Upland Way (SUW). This rises through fields before making its way across increasingly exposed moorland. After another 1km, the climb relents and the track heads across open moor, with the way ahead clearly visible. Off to the right with a prominent trig point at the summit is Bught Fell, while ahead and to the left is a windfarm. In front of Bught Fell is Kilhern Moss, dotted with hut circles and cairns.

When the track reaches the ruins of the old farmhouse of Kilhern (SUW sign here), it bends left before passing through a gate. Keep to the track as it goes through another gate and swings left again, with the windfarm now on the right. It weaves across moorland for a few hundred metres, passing a cutting of exposed rock and coming to a drystone wall and a wooden sign for the Caves of Kilhern.

Accompany the wall for around 200m to

◀ Caves of Kilhern

a fence: there is a surmountable wooden section (the rest of the wire fence is electrified), but it is best to follow the fenceline for a further 100m to a gate.

The caves are known to have been a chambered long cairn used as a communal burial place during Neolithic times. Although only four stone-lined chambers are visible, the site would originally have been 33m long. It has been extensively desecrated, so there is little known about the occupants or how they were buried.

Having finished the detour to the caves, carry on along the track to a junction

with two gates: go through the gate straight ahead to find the SUW sign beyond and drop downhill along the edge of the field, past a small wood. There are markers at points along the way. At the far side of the wood, the drystone wall bends away from the trail, which continues downhill to a farm track. Turn left onto this and follow it until it reaches a single-track road. A left onto the road takes you along the Cross Water of Luce and back to New Luce.

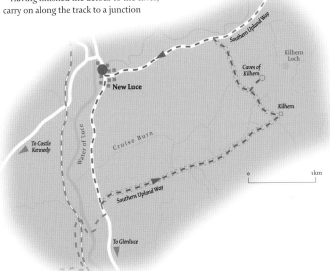

17

Glenluce Abbey and the Pilgrims Way

Distance 7.5km **Time** 2 hours
Terrain roads and paths; steep but brief
climb to start **Map** OS Landranger 82
Access bus (410) from Stranraer

**A delightful walk from Glenluce to the
atmospheric ruins of the abbey and then
along quiet roads that trace an ancient
pilgrimage route.**

In Glenluce, walk along the main road
to Church Street, which climbs steeply,
crossing a railway bridge. Proceed along
the narrow lane to a junction, where you
continue straight ahead. A short way
beyond the junction, where the road
bends right, cross a stile by a farm gate to
skirt along the edge of the field. The path
crosses another stile with a hedge to the
right, then a burn and a further stile.
In this field, keep the wall to your left.

Take the opportunity to pause and enjoy
views over the valley and towards the
South Rhins. Don't be alarmed by the
fact that at this point the route crosses
the Scotland-Ireland gas pipeline, which
runs for 135km from Twynholm, near
Kirkcudbright, to Ballylumford in
Northern Ireland.

The route then crosses another
stile/gate onto a track. Follow this to gain
access, via a gate, to a concrete single-
track road, which leads downhill and
meets the driveway for Glenluce Abbey.
Managed by Historic Scotland, the abbey
is well worth a visit: there is a charge for
entering the site. One of three abbeys in
Dumfries and Galloway (the others
are at Dundrennan and New Abbey),
Glenluce was founded in 1191 by Roland,
Lord of Galloway, and followed the

◄ Glenluce Abbey

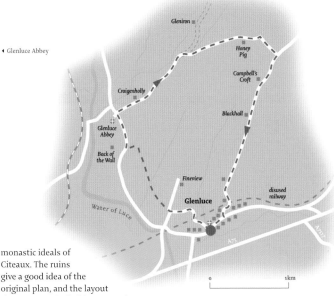

monastic ideals of Citeaux. The ruins give a good idea of the original plan, and the layout shows many similarities to Dundrennan Abbey further east and to Byland and Roche Abbeys in Yorkshire. The site is remote and tranquil, and even now gives a good sense of what life was like here when it was occupied.

From the abbey, you can either retrace your steps to Glenluce or complete the circuit by taking the single-track road, signposted Pilgrims Way, opposite the car park. This was one of many pilgrimage routes to Whithorn, this one used by royals making their way from Stirling, via Glasgow and Ayr; it is known to have been followed by Robert the Bruce,

James IV and Mary Queen of Scots.

The road climbs to a peak at the marvellously named house of Honey Pig. It then descends to a T-junction, where you turn right and follow the road downhill back to Glenluce. The views throughout this stage are splendid, offering a great panorama to the south. Although these roads are quiet, care should still be taken. The road eventually passes the Gospel Hall, where you turn right to return to the start point. Refreshments are available in Glenluce and Stranraer.

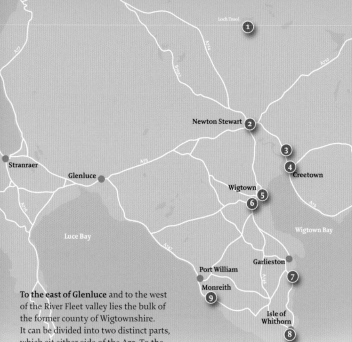

To the east of Glenluce and to the west of the River Fleet valley lies the bulk of the former county of Wigtownshire. It can be divided into two distinct parts, which sit either side of the A75. To the north are found hilly moorland and mountains, most of which lie within the Galloway Forest Park. This area is home to many of Southern Scotland's loftiest peaks, including the highest of all – the Merrick – which stands at 843m above sea level. The major settlement here is the market town of Newton Stewart, which is branded as the 'Gateway to the Galloway Hills' and is an excellent all-round base for coast and country.

South of the A75 is the wide peninsula of gently undulating farmland and heath known as the Machars (thought to be from the Gaelic *Machair* – 'low lying').

The long coastline offers sandy bays, spectacular cliffs and wildlife-rich mudflats, as well as plenty of history.

Not far from Newton Stewart, at the entrance to the Machars, sits Wigtown, best known as Scotland's Book Town. Dotted around the coast are a number of pretty towns, including Creetown, Garlieston, Port William and the Isle of Whithorn, all of which make good bases for exploring Wigtownshire. Tranquility and solitude can be found in abundance here – as can the most southerly distillery in Scotland.

Port William ▶

Galloway Forest to the Machars

Mull of Galloway
New York 3540
Newcastle 431m
Belfast

Loop of Loch Trool

Distance 8km **Time** 2 hours 30
Terrain waymarked but undulating and
muddy paths **Map** OS Landranger 77
Access A714 to Bargrennan, then the Glen
Trool village road to the visitor centre
and beyond to Bruce's Stone (signed)

**This is an atmospheric walk in the depths
of the Galloway Forest with a Highland
air and an abundance of history.**

Start from the public car park near the
Bruce's Stone, Glen Trool. This route is
waymarked (green posts with a green
band), but is walked in the opposite
direction to the arrows on the posts.
Although the trail is well maintained,
walking boots and gaiters are highly
recommended, as it can get muddy.

From the car park, follow the footpath
into the heather to find Bruce's Stone.

This boulder commemorates the famous
Battle of Glen Trool. Across the loch on 31
March 1307, Robert the Bruce led 300 Scots
to ambush an English patrol of 1500,
which had been dispatched to find Bruce,
a fugitive following the defeat of the Scots
army at The Battle of Methven in 1306.
Despite their disadvantage in number, the
Scots pushed boulders down the steep
hill, throwing many into the loch and
then used archers to complete the victory.

Simply return to the car park from the
memorial and bear right along the tarmac
track (waymarked as National Cycle
Network Route 7) as it swings right and
descends. The track then crosses an old
stone bridge over the wonderful gorge of
the Buchan Burn. Once across the bridge,
take the left fork (signposted Gairland
Burn), crossing a wooden bridge when

◄ Loch Trool

you reach the burn. Some 400m further on, a footpath (still Route 7) branches right. Follow this to reach a four-way wooden signpost, where you turn right and cross a wooden footbridge: go straight ahead uphill on the Southern Upland Way. The path swings right and undulates as it traverses the steep hillside at the southern edge of the loch, with views across the water from time to time, passing an informative plaque which commemorates the battle and then drawing nearer to the loch for more views.

After around 2km, the path leaves the hillside and enters a meadow where you turn left onto a cinder track and cross a concrete bridge. Turn right at the next junction and right again after 100m to cross two bridges 200m apart, bringing you to a small car park, site of the former Caldons Campsite.

Take the signposted Loch Trool Forest Trail from the back of the car park to weave through a felled area with good views before diving into a wood. After 50m in the trees, the waymarked trail bends left and a faint path continues ahead. Follow this path for a gradual climb away from the loch. At the road, turn right to return to the start.

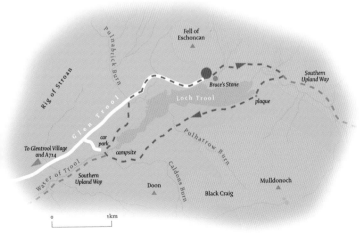

Newton Stewart on the Cree

Distance 3km **Time** 1 hour
Terrain buggy-friendly pavements
Map OS Landranger 83 **Access** bus (415)
from the Machars, (416) from Whithorn
and Stranraer, (431, 517) from Gatehouse
and Kirkcudbright, (500) from Stranraer
and Dumfries

**Explore a traditional market town
and the River Cree which runs through it.**

The bustling market town of Newton
Stewart originally developed through
medieval times as a crossing point over
the River Cree; Robert the Bruce crossed
here in 1329 on a pilgrimage to Whithorn.
In 1677, the new town on the west side of
the Cree was joined with Minnigaff on
the east to form the Burgh of Barony
of Newton Stewart, allowing the town
to hold the weekly markets and annual
fairs that would contribute to its growing
prosperity and development as a site
for the manufacture of woollen goods.
The town is now more associated with
tourism, as it is ideally located for access
to the Galloway Hills for walkers and
mountain bikers. In the 1790s, local
entrepreneur William Douglas tried
to change the name of the town to
Newton Douglas; having failed, he moved
further east where he had more success in
the renaming of Castle Douglas.

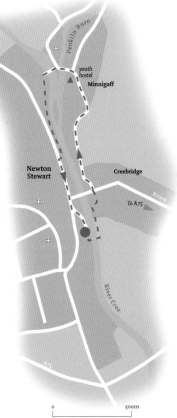

◀ Bridge over the Cree

From the riverside car park in Newton Stewart, cross Sparling Bridge, so named after a rare fish found in the River Cree, and turn left to follow the east bank of the river. After around 400m, the road bends away from the river to meet a residential road, where a left turn takes you to a crossroads. Looking left, you'll see the Cree Bridge, built in 1812-13 from local granite. The weir was constructed to protect the bridge foundations. Go straight ahead at the crossroads, passing the youth hostel and a war memorial before reaching a Y-junction. Take the branch to the left to cross the Penkiln Burn. Where the road swings right, turn left to cross a pedestrian suspension bridge over the Cree (both rivers join within a few metres of the bridges).

The pedestrian bridge leads into a park, a good spot to pause and enjoy the river and woodland. Now follow the concrete path off to the left to head up a ramp and continue down the road through some new houses. At the end of the road, turn left and follow this back to the high street. After passing the Cree Bridge, take the first left onto Riverside Road to return to the car park by the footbridge at the start.

Cairnsmore of Fleet

Distance 12.5km **Time** 3 hours 45
Terrain muddy footpaths, tracks and
roads; fairly long and unrelenting climb
Map OS Landranger 83 **Access** bus (431)
from Newton Stewart or Gatehouse of
Fleet (stops at Palnure, approximately
1km from start)

This longer route goes through an old
country estate, into dense forest and over
moorland, rewarding the effort with
magnificent views across Galloway and
the Solway. This is a hill walk, so go
prepared with map and compass (and
the ability to use them) and clothing
appropriate for variable weather.

Cairnsmore of Fleet is the most
southerly of the three Cairnsmore peaks
in Dumfries and Galloway, the others
being Cairnsmore of Dee and Cairnsmore
of Carsphairn. At 711m, it is smaller than

Cairnsmore of Carsphairn but still makes
for an exhilarating climb.

To get to the start, turn off the A75 at
Muirfad, which is near Palnure, between
Creetown (4km) and Newton Stewart
(5km), heading past a disused railway
bridge and taking the next right into the
signposted car park on the edge of the
Cairnsmore Estate. At the far end of the
car park, walk through a metal gate, turn
left and follow the road, keeping the river
to your right. After a couple of minutes of
road walking, you will see a signpost
marked 'Hill Path' which directs you onto
a waymarked footpath through a small
wood. Where the path meets a track, turn
left to access a metal gate into a field.

On entering the field, head towards the
far right corner at a 45-degree angle on a
rising course, where you will see a gate in
the wall at the top of the field. Go through

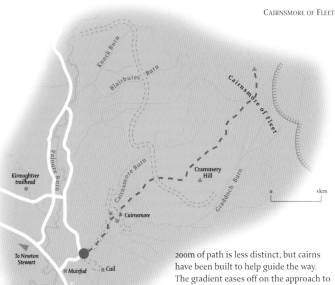

this gate into another wood, crossing a stile (signposted for the summit) and a small burn. Beyond the burn, follow the path and signposts uphill onto a muddy track which gives a long climb through the forest. After around 500m, this reaches a track and small clearing, a welcome chance to catch your breath and take in the view.

The climb continues and, after passing through a gate and stile, the forest will become a distant memory as you strike out onto open moorland for another 2.5km slog. For most of the journey, the path is clear and easy to follow. The last

200m of path is less distinct, but cairns have been built to help guide the way. The gradient eases off on the approach to the top, which can mislead you into thinking the top is closer than it is. The summit is marked by a cairn, a trig point and a memorial to the aircraft and their crews who have crashed on this mountain. These include RAF, USAF and German aircrews from WWII and the 1950s. Some of the crashed aircraft came from the nearby airfield by Wigtown – it is now disused but visible on maps – and remnants can be seen on the ground. The three features are positioned in a triangle across the plateau, each giving a different perspective of the landscape. Once you have soaked up the views, simply retrace your steps to the start. For refreshments, the Kirroughtree mountain biking centre, by Palnure, has a café, otherwise there are plenty of options in Newton Stewart.

◀ From the summit of Cairnsmore of Fleet

Cairnsmore to Creetown

Distance 5km (one-way) **Time** 1 hour 30 (one-way) **Terrain** tarmac paths, roads and dirt tracks; buggy-friendly as far as Creetown road (round-trip 6km to retrace steps from here) **Map** OS Landranger 83 **Access** bus (431) from Newton Stewart, Gatehouse of Fleet and Kirkcudbright; (500) from Stranraer and Dumfries (both stop at Palnure, 1km from start, and can be used for the return from Creetown)

Follow a disused railway line – now a Sustrans cycle track – that passes through glorious Galloway countryside with views across to Wigtown and over the bay.

Start from the layby near the end of the driveway to Cuil. To get here by car, turn off the A75 at Muirfad, which is near Palnure, between Creetown (4km) and

Newton Stewart (5km), and follow the minor road to the entrance to Cuil. The cycle track starts here at the metal gate next to the layby, and is signposted: it is part of National Route 7, which runs for 630km from Carlisle to Inverness. Space is limited: an alternative is to park at the Cairnsmore car park (*see p26*).

Walk through the gate and follow the tarmac track as it rises gently through woods, passes through an old railway cutting and then under power lines. The path eventually leaves the trees and climbs to a blue Sustrans post, a good place to stop and enjoy the views across the bay and west towards Newton Stewart.

This cycle route follows the line of the old Portpatrick Railway, completed in 1861. It ran for 85km to Castle Douglas, and Creetown had its own station about

◀ Downtown Creetown

Muirfad Cuil

To Palnure
and Newton
Stewart

Blairs

Pulwhat Burn

1km

Carsewalloch

River Cree

Spittal

Lennies

Moneypool Burn

Barholm
Mains

Creetown

2km north of the town. As it continues, the trail drops down from and then returns to the embankment, passing through two gates in between. Eventually, it goes through a farm (to return from this point is around an hour-long 3.5km walk). A few hundred metres further on, the track starts to descend to a road leading into Creetown.

Where the cycleway joins the road beyond a gate and cattle grid, turn left for an on-road stretch which passes two parking areas and comes to a farm gate (marked with a green footpath sign) on the right after around 500m.

Go through the gate to accompany the track as it swings right and descends, then bends left towards some houses and begins to run parallel to the A75. Another farm gate leads you into deciduous woodland, then you turn right to follow a gravel track (again marked with the green footpath sign), which goes through a wooden gate and past more houses on the left before becoming a road. The road bends right, takes you over the Moneypool Burn and arrives at the square in the small town of Creetown, where you'll find refreshments.

Creetown initially developed as a ferry crossing over the mouth of the River Cree for pilgrims to Whithorn, and its original name was Ferrytown of Cree. Local granite quarries, such as nearby Kirkmabreck, brought prosperity to the area. It is said that Kirkmabreck-quarried granite helped to build Liverpool, Swansea and Greenock docks.

Wigtown and the Martyrs' Stake

Distance 3km **Time** 1 hour
Terrain paved roads and muddy paths;
check tide times before venturing out to
Martyrs' Stake **Map** OS Landranger 83
Access bus (415) from Newton Stewart

**Take your time to explore Scotland's
National Book Town, whose civilised air
belies a sometimes bloody history.**

You may not find Wigtown quite so
sedate during its annual autumn literary
festival, though this is a great time to visit
for the friendly atmosphere and many
events: book well in advance. When you're
done with browsing the town's dozen or
so bookshops, start the walk from the
county buildings (including the town hall
and library), which can be found at the
northern end of the high street and
identified by the distinctive clocktower.

Facing the front of the county buildings,
follow Bank Street around the left-hand
side to drop downhill past a churchyard.
A signposted detour leads to the graves of
the Wigtown Martyrs, two women who
were condemned to death by drowning in
the nearby marsh during the Killing
Times of the 1680s. During this period,
large numbers of Covenanters were
hunted down and executed by
government soldiers because of their
refusal to accept the Crown's interference
in their worship. The graves are towards
the back of the churchyard, encircled
by iron railings.

Carry on along the road to a
parking and picnic area, where
you turn right to follow the
old railway line along the
edge of the marsh: it is

all well signposted. After around 50m, the path reaches an interpretation board and a trail out into the marsh. Follow the trail to the monument known as the Martyrs' Stake, where the two women were said to have been left to face the rising tide. **Please note, the area is highly tidal and care should be taken when venturing out onto the marsh.**

The path continues past the monument with great views across Wigtown Bay and over the saltmarsh. On the far shoreline is Kirkmabreck Quarry: stone from here was used to build many harbours across Britain, including Liverpool and Greenock.

Leaving the old railway line, the path drops down off the embankment and meets a gate onto a single-track road. Turn left to follow the road to the harbour: it was restored in the 1980s, but throughout its history Wigtown never developed as a trading port because the harbour was vulnerable to silting.

From here, go left along a track if you wish to visit the bird hide. This highly tidal low-lying area is a local nature reserve, the saltmarsh providing a rich habitat for many migratory birds including pink-footed geese, which overwinter here, and also to breeds such as lapwing, redshank, pintail and swans.

To return to the start, retrace your steps up the road to the junction with the old pathway, continuing along the road to the 30mph signs, where you turn right. This road leads back uphill towards the clocktower.

◂ In Wigtown's triangular Square

Bladnoch riverside trail

Distance 3.5km **Time** 1 hour 30
Terrain buggy-friendly cinder track to
viewing platform, then muddy path with
some narrow, exposed sections
Map OS Landranger 83 **Access** bus (415)
from Newton Stewart

From Bladnoch Distillery, enjoy a
gentle riverside stroll with plenty of
wildlife-spotting opportunities along
the way.

The walk starts from the distillery car
park, which is located southwest of
Wigtown off the A714. Leave the far end of
the car park through a gap between the
cottage and distillery building, next to
a 'Welcome' sign. Here, a path leads across
a lawn to a cinder track: it may feel like
you're tramping through someone's
back garden, but this is the recognised
route out of the distillery grounds.
The path runs between the tidal lower
reaches of the River Bladnoch, which
empties into the sea at Wigtown, and a
man-made lade, which diverts river water
from above the tidal range into the
distillery: it gives the walk a magical
feeling reminiscent of Madeira's famous
Lavada (waterway) trails.

A meander through peaceful mixed
woodland leads to a viewing platform,
where you can see trout feeding on flies
and salmon jumping as they approach
their spawning grounds. The river is also a
haven for grey heron and mute swans,
and is alleged to be home to a lone otter.

◄ Bladnoch Distillery

This also marks the end of the purpose-built cinder path, suitable for buggies: if turning around at this point, the total length of the walk is 1.5km.

From here, the path can be muddy and care should be taken as there are some narrow sections with drops on either side. The dirt path continues to a weir, which you will hear before you see; a concrete section marks the beginning of this. From the weir, it simply remains to retrace your steps to the distillery. On the return, the path gives a good view of the bridge by the start point, which was built in 1860 and made of local stone. It replaced a wooden bridge originally designed to help pilgrims on their way to Whithorn.

Refreshments are available near the distillery and in Wigtown or Newton Stewart. The distillery tour is worth joining and there is a whisky shop. In the visitor centre, there is a curling stone that has been hewn from the quarry on Ailsa Craig, the granite island located at the mouth of Loch Ryan. The distillery was established in 1817 and at its peak, in the 1850s, produced over 51,000 gallons of whisky. The site was owned by United Distillers when it was closed in 1993; it was bought in 1995 and reopened in 2000. Bladnoch Distillery has very strong local links and plays host to a variety of events, including an annual river rafting day.

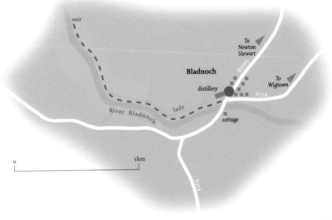

Cruggleton Castle clifftop walk

Distance 8.5km **Time** 2 hours
Terrain muddy paths; gentle slopes with
some exposure **Map** OS Landranger 83
Access bus (415) from Newton Stewart,
(416) from Stranraer

A walk through woodland and across
cliffs to visit the ruins of an ancient
castle, returning through the grounds of
a once magnificent country estate.

Start at the public car park opposite the
village hall in Garlieston. From here,
continue along the road as it passes
between two caravan parks and leads into
the old harbour. Where the road
eventually reaches the breakwater, take a
dirt track to the right. After around 300m,
the track meets a metal gate, which you
go through to continue along the
footpath, meandering along the sea edge
and through trees. Some 800m further on,
at a green hut with a good view across

Rigg Bay, the path splits: take the left-
hand option. On the walk to this point,
the magnificent classical mansion of
Galloway House can be glimpsed through
the trees. The remnants of a Mulberry
harbour from WWII once sat in the bay;
however, storms have finally removed this
feature (for more details, there are
information boards in Garlieston).

The path runs across the back of Rigg
Bay and joins a larger trail after a small
right and left turn. Carry on around the
bay on this path, passing a picnic site,
signs to a woodland walk, a ruined
cottage and over two bridged burns.
The path now starts to lead gently uphill
and into wonderful deciduous woodland
until it reaches a cliff edge, marked by a
bench. The small arch visible on the
horizon is part of the castle ruins.
Depending on the season, this part of
the route will be flanked by fields of

◄ Looking out from
Crugleton Castle

bluebells, dog's mercury
or wild garlic.

As the path continues, it
passes through an iron gate to
the left of a cottage and skirts along
exposed cliffs. The landscape now
changes from woodland to open
fields. Turn through a wall into
a field, following the signposted
path along the edge of three
fields to Cruggleton Castle.
The remains of the ancient
castle can be reached over a
stile and enjoys views in all
directions. It was built in
the 13th century by the
Lords of Galloway on the
site of an Iron Age fort
and is said to have
featured in the Scottish Wars of
Independence, being taken by both
William Wallace and Edward I.
It was eventually destroyed and the stone
used for local buildings. Located in a
copse to the west of the castle, though no
longer accessible from it, is Cruggleton
Church, built in the 13th century for the
castle's residents.

Retrace your steps to Rigg Bay. At a
picnic area with stone plinth and two
wooden benches, take the tarmac track to
the left. This goes through a farm gate,
past cottages and a walled garden. At the
end of the walled garden, take the right-
hand path, signed for the car park. From
the car park, follow the exit road, which

gives wonderful views of Galloway House,
built in 1740 by Lord Alexander Garlies,
son of the fifth Earl of Galloway.

At a crossroads after around 300m, go
straight on over a cattle grid. This road
leads over another cattle grid into a farm
courtyard. Continue through this to meet
a dirt track, then turn left onto this to
cross open fields and eventually emerge
near the caravan park in Garlieston. Go
through a gate in the stone wall and turn
left to retrace your steps to the start.

35

Isle of Whithorn and Burrow Head

Distance 9km **Time** 2 hours 30
Terrain tarmac and muddy paths with
some exposure **Map** OS Landranger 83
Access bus (415) from Newton Stewart

**From the home of Scotland's first saint,
take this clifftop pilgrimage to a
headland made famous by the 1970's cult
horror film *The Wicker Man*.**

Start this walk from the harbour car
park in the Isle of Whithorn, a truly lovely
village which, however, no longer lays
claim to being an island, owing to its
causeway built in the 1790s and later
developed. The village first grew as a port
for pilgrims on their way to the town of
Whithorn – home to Scotland's first saint,
St Ninian – but later as a centre for trade
and smuggling.

The route is well signposted with the
Dumfries & Galloway green and yellow
footpath signs. However, it can feel

exposed in places and will not suit the
less sure-footed. From the car park, walk
back up the road to reach a footpath off to
the left (signed to Burrow Head). Go
through the kissing gate at the far end
and cross the field, keeping to the path as
it passes through a number of gates and
fields, and goes over a wooden footbridge.

The path slowly climbs until it emerges
out of the fields to run along the cliff
edge. The views are spectacular, with the
Isle of Whithorn in the foreground and
the Solway coast stretching away beyond.

Eventually, the path passes a well-
preserved WWII pillbox and a bit further
on turns a corner, bringing Burrowhead
caravan site into view ahead. As the path
turns another corner, you'll see the
remains of an ancient hill fort to the right.
Continue to follow the signs as the path
leaves the cliff edge for the caravan site.
At the signpost to St Ninian's Cave, turn

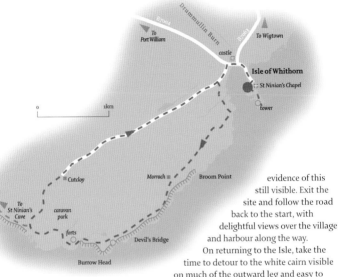

To Port William

To Wigtown

castle

Isle of Whithorn

St Ninian's Chapel

tower

0   1km

Cutcloy

Morrach

Broom Point

To St Ninian's Cave

caravan park

forts

Devil's Bridge

Burrow Head

left and follow the path as it skirts around the caravans. (Believed to have been St Ninian's retreat, the cave was more recently the site of the beach scene in the 1973 film *The Wicker Man*. Located on the far side of the pebbly Port Castle Bay, it marks an eerie end to a long, lonely clifftop detour from Burrow Head.) After crossing a small burn, the path reaches a signposted junction with a red bench, where you turn right to leave the cliffs, following the tarmac track through the caravan site to the main entrance. While skirting the caravan site, the walk has crossed the location for a number of other scenes from *The Wicker Man*, including the final burning scene. The site was also home to a WWII army training camp, with

evidence of this still visible. Exit the site and follow the road back to the start, with delightful views over the village and harbour along the way.

On returning to the Isle, take the time to detour to the white cairn visible on much of the outward leg and easy to find from the car park. For more than two centuries, it was used to help boats navigate this coast. On your way to the cairn, you will pass a memorial dedicated to the local men who lost their lives when the fishing vessel, the *Solway Harvester*, sank off the Isle of Man in 2000, a sad reminder of the part the sea plays in life here.

From the car park, the route out to the headland also passes St Ninian's Chapel, thought to have been built around 1300 to assist pilgrims arriving by sea to visit the religious centre of Whithorn, some 5km to the northwest. It was extensively rebuilt in 1898 but occupies the site of the original chapel. Many of the houses in the village are thought to have been built using stone from the original building.

◀ The harbour at Isle of Whithorn

Monreith and the Fell of Barhullion

Distance 6km **Time** 1 hour 45
Terrain Paved roads, dirt tracks and
muddy paths; gentle climb, steep at end
Map OS Landranger 83 **Access** bus (415)
from Newton Stewart, (416) from Newton
Stewart and Stranraer

This is a superb walk through the history
of a delightful village up to the summit
of the Fell of Barhullion. For a hill of
modest height, it offers a fantastic
panorama of the region.

Start at the public car park at the Back
Bay of Monreith village. Return along the
road towards the village, stopping to look
at the ruins of Kirkmaiden Church, one of
Scotland's oldest churches, which is set
into the hillside with lively associations
to a number of legends and omens. The
graveyard contains tombs of the families

who originally owned the Monreith
Estate. Continue uphill until you reach a
bronze otter which stands on the rocks
beside the road. This is a monument to
the author Gavin Maxwell, best known for
his book *Ring of Bright Water*, who grew up
in nearby Monreith House. The monument
occupies the site of his favourite view.

From here, take the path signposted to
Clarksburn. This runs across the clifftop
and then passes through two wooden
gates to follow an old drystone wall to the
edge of a wood. Enter this by a wooden
gate and exit via another gate onto the
A-road into Monreith. Cross the road and
follow the track up the other side of the
burn, signed for the Fell of Barhullion: the
summit is visible ahead. For around 1km,
the track passes houses and fields
bounded by drystone walls, with small

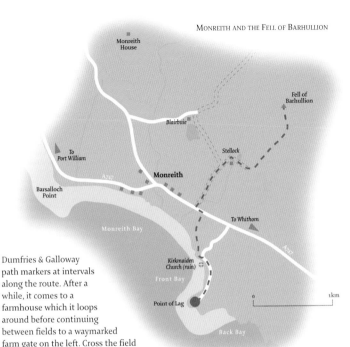

Dumfries & Galloway path markers at intervals along the route. After a while, it comes to a farmhouse which it loops around before continuing between fields to a waymarked farm gate on the left. Cross the field beyond the gate, exiting at the top.

From here, walk across a second field to reach a rocky outcrop surrounded by gorse. The summit has a cairn and trig point, and offers a fantastic panorama of the region. Starting from the south, there's the Isle of Man, then turning to the right are the small islands in the Solway known as the Scares: these are used by the RAF for bombing practice. Going right again is the lighthouse on the Mull of Galloway and the eastern coast of the South Rhins. From here the eye is drawn along the beautiful coast of the Machars to the windfarm near New Luce,

the Galloway Hills and the coastal hills to the east (which include Cairnsmore of Fleet, Bengairn and Criffel), then the eastern end of the Solway and the Cumbrian coast and Lake District peaks.

The best route of return is to simply retrace your steps to the start. It is well worth visiting the sandy beaches after this walk to appreciate a lovely stretch of coast hidden from view on Barhullion. Refreshments are available at Monreith Animal World (seasonal) on the A747 towards Whithorn or in Whithorn itself.

◀ Memorial to the author Gavin Maxwell

The routes in this chapter sit broadly within the boundaries of the River Fleet catchment to the west and the Ken/Dee river system to the east. The Ken/Dee valley has been developed into a huge hydro-electric scheme, which has created some great recreation and birdspotting opportunities – not least at Loch Ken, a reservoir for the hydro scheme and a magnet for watersports enthusiasts.

From the southern edge of Loch Ken to the Ayrshire border is the Glenkens – literally 'The Valley of the Ken'. It is Galloway's largest and wildest glen, and so under-visited that little has changed since 1721 when Sir John Clerk of Penicuik lauded its 'mountains wild beyond imagination so that scarce any thing in the Alps exceeds them'. It offers fantastic scenery and walking of all levels.

The main settlements in this area are the beautiful towns of New Galloway and further north, on the River Dee, St John's Town of Dalry (usually known as Dalry). The latter was developed by the Knights Hospitaller of the order of St John of Jerusalem as a stop-off for pilgrims from Edinburgh visiting Whithorn and the shrine to St Ninian.

To the south, set in the more gentle landscape that rolls down towards the Solway Firth in the designated National Scenic Area of the Fleet Valley, is one of the best-loved destinations for visitors to Galloway – Gatehouse of Fleet. Like New Galloway and Dalry, Gatehouse is ideally situated for access to the Galloway Forest and Loch Ken, but it is also superbly sited to access the ample coastline of the area.

The Glenkens to Gatehouse

St John's Town of Dalry pilgrimage

Distance **4km** Time **1 hour 30**
Terrain **narrow, muddy paths and paved
roads** Map **OS Landranger 77**
Access **bus (520) from Castle Douglas and
Ayr, (521) from Dumfries**

**An easy riverside walk from St John's
Town of Dalry, which follows the
Southern Upland Way to the summit of
Waterside Hill, taking in a hydro-electric
power station along the way and giving
great views along the River Ken Valley.**

Located north of New Galloway,
St John's Town of Dalry developed to
service the needs of pilgrims travelling to
Whithorn from Edinburgh. The Knights
Hospitaller of the order of St John of
Jerusalem owned the land and created a
settlement to help pilgrims cross the river
and offer accommodation. James IV of
Scotland was one pilgrim who is known

to have travelled this route. Today, Dalry –
as it is locally known – is a lovely village
which remains an important staging post,
though this time for travellers on the
long-distance Southern Upland Way.

Start the walk in the middle of Dalry,
facing the town hall, which is set back
from a T-junction. Take the path,
signposted for the Southern Upland Way
(SUW), which runs along the right-hand
side of the town hall and drops down to
the river at a suspension bridge. Cross the
bridge which – those of nervous
disposition should be warned – does
wobble alarmingly, and follow the path
off to the right as it skirts the riverbank.

The route takes you through a kissing

gate, over a burn and on a meander through some trees, before passing through another gate to eventually reach the road. Turn right onto this, then follow the SUW sign off to the left and walk up the track to a metal farm gate, with the power station and the impressive salmon ladders to the right.

Beyond the gate, the SUW takes you through a field. Around 150m after passing under a powerline, look right to see the summit cairn of Waterside Hill. At a suitable point, head towards this. On gaining the summit, you will have views over Dalry, along the Ken Valley, over the power station and to the distant hills of Corserine to the north, Cairnsmore of Carsphairn further to the east and Bengairn to the south.

To return, retrace your steps to the road, turning left to pass in front of Earsltoun Power Station. This is part of the Galloway Hydro scheme, completed in 1935, which consists of seven dams and six generating stations that stretch along the Ken-Dee river system. A dam located 500m north of the power station has raised Earsltoun Loch to a level that can supply the power

station with enough water. On the walk, the salmon ladders, pipework and other features of the power station are visible. The hydro scheme is still operated by the original turbines, and supplies the area with power nearly 80 years after being built.

Beyond the power station, cross a concrete bridge. At a T-junction, turn right and cross the bridge over the River Ken to follow the road on a gentle meander back to Dalry. The road is bordered by paths along most of its length, but you will need to cross from side to side periodically. Refreshments are available in Dalry, and the town itself is well worth exploring.

◀ The Clachan Inn, St John's Town of Dalry

New Galloway and Kenmure Holms

Distance 4km **Time** 1 hour 30
Terrain narrow, muddy paths and paved
roads **Map** OS Landranger 77
Access bus (520) from Castle Douglas and
Ayr, (521) from Dumfries

**Explore a protected wildlife habitat on
the edge of the River Ken before
returning to delightful New Galloway.**

Start the walk from the Carson Knowe
car park on the edge of New Galloway,
which is down a single-track road. From
the far end of the car park, a clearly
signposted path follows the burn. It is
very easy to follow as it runs along the
top of an embankment, with occasional
interpretive boards along the way. The
Kenmure Holms Nature Reserve is the
furthest south of its type in Scotland and
supports a wide range of wildlife, large
and small. A designated Site of Special
Scientific Interest (SSSI), it is an
internationally important site for

overwintering greylag and Greenland
geese; it also contains a number of rare
plants and insects, including an
outstanding range of dragonflies. This
route traverses the northern end of the
reserve. Please note, the area can be prone
to rapid flooding, so it is advisable to stay
on the embankment path.

Depending on the time of year, the
route enjoys occasional glimpses of the
ruins of Kenmure Castle. It is thought
that the site has been occupied since the
12th century, but part of the castle dates
from the 16th century. It was built on an
outcrop to dominate the low-lying land
and is visible from the surrounding roads.
Sadly, the castle was abandoned in the
1950s: opinions are divided over whether
it fell victim to a fire or the deliberate
removal of the roof to avoid roof tax.

The path trends left around part of the
swamp area, eventually coming to a gate.
Pass through this to begin the return leg,

◀ Reed bank in Kenmure Holms

now with the river on your right. After around 500m, you'll pass a path off to the left which runs between two fences and crosses a field towards New Galloway. For a shorter 2km route, which should take just over half an hour, you can follow this path all the way back to the car park. Otherwise, carry on along the embankment path for the longer route to Ken Bridge. Completed in 1824, it was constructed from grey granite and consists of five arches. Pass under the bridge and immediately turn left to join the road. Here, you can take a left to detour to the hotel for refreshments or turn right to return to the car park. Follow the meanders of the A712, also known as the Old Edinburgh Road, to the edge of New Galloway and turn left onto the single-track road to return to the start. On the way, you can make a detour into the park to view the large granite war memorial which is on an impressive scale given the size of the town. With its pleasant,

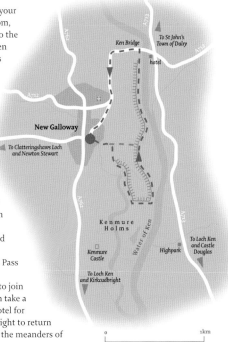

secluded air, New Galloway's position on the fringes of the Galloway Forest makes it a good base for forest walks: you can take the Queen's Way west past Clatteringshaws Loch to Newton Stewart or go south to Loch Ken, a hub for water-based activities, and beyond to the coast.

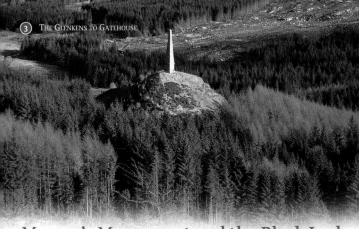

Murray's Monument and the Black Loch

Distance 5km **Time** 1 hour 30
Terrain gravel and muddy tracks; paths
shared with mountain bikers, two river
crossings **Map** OS Landranger 77
Access no public transport

**This is a magnificent walk from Talnotry
in the Galloway Forest, offering
waterfalls, sculpture and the chance to
walk along an ancient pilgrimage route.**

Start from the Grey Mare's Tail car park
in the Galloway Forest, off The Queen's
Way (A712) between New Galloway (16km)
and Newton Stewart (12km). Look out for
mountain bikers on the smaller paths and
take care on the two burn crossings: you
may not be able to complete the Black
Loch circuit after heavy rain. The forest is
a haven for wildlife and on any given day
peregrine falcons, golden eagle and even
hen harriers can be seen in the area, along
with roe and red deer and feral goats: the
goats are thought to have been released

when land clearances took place in the
18th and 19th centuries.

Leave the car park and follow the clear
path up to the stone needle above. This is
Murray's Monument, erected in memory
of a local shepherd boy and self-taught
linguist who went on to become professor
of oriental languages at Edinburgh
University in the 1800s. The monument
affords great views of Cairnsmore of Fleet,
along the valley and to the Goat Range.

Retrace your steps as far as a green post
with red band, then follow this path
around until it meets another path, where
you should turn right to climb uphill.
When this eventually reaches a forest
track, turn right along this to go through
woodland and across a concrete bridge.
Detour left along the far bank to follow a
faint path to the wonderful sight of the
Grey Mare's Tail waterfall.

Simply return to the concrete bridge
and continue along the forest track: this is

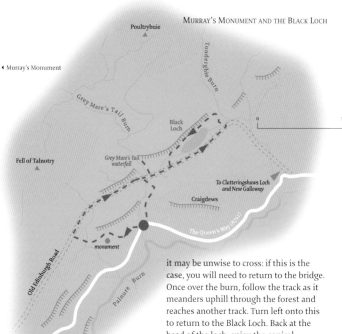

◀ Murray's Monument

Poultrybuie ▲

Tonderghie Burn

Grey Mare's Tail Burn

Black Loch

Fell of Talnotry ▲

Grey Mare's Tail waterfall

To Clatteringshaws Loch and New Galloway

Craigdews

The Queen's Way (A712)

monument ●

Old Edinburgh Road

Palnure Burn

To Newton Stewart

0   1k

the old Edinburgh Road used by pilgrims to Whithorn. At the head of the Black Loch, the track comes to a junction. Follow the right-hand route as it skirts around the loch. After passing the foot of the loch and going through a metal barrier, turn left and follow a path down towards a burn. Pick a point to cross the burn – there are numerous stepping stones – and then climb uphill away from it to a grassy forestry track. Turn left along this to head downhil, crossing a smaller burn by stepping stones. After heavy rain,

it may be unwise to cross: if this is the case, you will need to return to the bridge. Once over the burn, follow the track as it meanders uphill through the forest and reaches another track. Turn left onto this to return to the Black Loch. Back at the head of the loch, enjoy the conical sculpture, then retrace your steps to the concrete bridge. Here, a red waymarker post points the way: turn left onto a cinder path into a sheepfold, looking out for faint sculptures hewn out of the stone. Exit the fold to accompany the burn for a few metres, before a path leaves the water and passes through a gap in a drystone wall. Once through the gap, follow the waymarkers up a small hill and then down the other side on a path that leads back to the start: refreshments are available at Clatteringshaws Visitor Centre (seasonal) and New Galloway to the east, or Newton Stewart to the west.

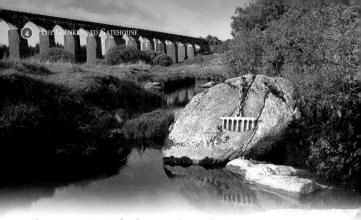

Big Water of Fleet circular

Distance 15km Time 3 hours
Terrain forestry tracks, gentle slopes
Map OS Landranger 83
Access no public transport

A circular walk that passes under the Big Water of Fleet viaduct on good tracks in a remote part of the Galloway Forest – with solitude and wildlife in abundance.

Start at the Scottish Natural Heritage (SNH) visitor centre at Dromore. To reach this, take the scenic B796 from Gatehouse of Fleet to Gatehouse Station – 10km from the town it once served – and turn right at the T-junction. Note, it is advisable to check if there are any forest operations in the area before setting out (visit www.forestry.gov.uk/forestry). It is also a good route on which to mountain bike or ride a horse. There are no refreshments near this route; the nearest shops and restaurants are in Gatehouse of Fleet.

From the visitor centre, follow the track towards the Big Water of Fleet Viaduct, which you pass under, and continue towards the forest. This viaduct once formed part of the Portpatrick and Wigtownshire railway, known as the Port Road, which provided the main link between England and the Irish ferry ports of Portpatrick and Stranraer. The rail link opened in the 1870s and was closed in the mid-1960s. The viaduct also featured in the original film of the John Buchan novel *The 39 Steps*.

The track eventually crosses a cattle grid and enters the forest, where it reaches a junction after 300m. Follow the track to the right, signed for Loch Grannoch Lodge, crossing a concrete bridge and, after a further 100m, turning right again at a junction. As this track gently curves to the left and gains height, good views of Cairnsmore of Fleet develop to your left. After a few minutes, the track levels off and straightens out as it joins the route of the old railway line.

It continues in this manner for 3km,

◀ Big Water of Fleet Viaduct

passing through cuttings and over embankments with views of recent forest operations along the way. A sudden sharp left, followed by a curve to the right begins the descent to cross a concrete bridge over the Little Water of Fleet.

Some 50m further on from the bridge, you'll come to a junction, where you turn left for a gentle ascent alongside the Little Water of Fleet. At a junction after 1.5km, take a left and then another left at a junction 1km further on, this time signposted for 'Loch Fleet, 2 miles'.

Immediately after turning, cross a concrete bridge and climb for 750m in distance to a track junction, taking the left here. A 500m stretch is followed by another left turn. The path now starts to descend and the countryside opens up to give good views of Cairnsmore of Fleet. After 2.5km, this track reaches a junction, where you take a left to follow the National Route 7 cycle sign. When you

reach another junction 200m further on, continue straight ahead. This should be familiar now as the route has rejoined the earlier section.

Continue along the track, cross the concrete bridge and take a left at the next track junction to emerge from the forest. Retrace the outward route under the viaduct and back to the visitor centre.

On the Anwoth trail

Distance **5km** Time **1 hour 30**
Terrain **roads and muddy footpaths**
Map **OS Landranger 83**
Access **bus (431, 517) from Newton
Stewart and Kirkcudbright, (500) from
Dumfries and Stranraer**

**Visit a landmark monument before
returning to Gatehouse of Fleet via an old
ruined church, made famous for its part
in a 1970's cult classic horror film.**

Start at the main public car park in
Gatehouse of Fleet, opposite the entrance
to the Mill on the Fleet. From the car park,
head back onto the road, turn left and
cross the bridge over the River Fleet.
Continue along this road as it leaves the
town until you see the sign for a footpath
to Anwoth at a sharp left bend: turn right
here. (You can take a detour here through
a wooden gate into a field to climb to the
top of Vinniehill: this gives marvellous

views over the town and area.)

On the right after 100m is another
optional detour along a short nature
trail, which follows boardwalks through a
man-made hollow that is now a wetland
habitat called Brickworks Field. The
hollow was made from extracting the clay
for brick-making in the 18th century and
is rich in wildflowers such as flag iris and
climbing marsh bedstraw.

As the road rises, it passes a bench and a
small green before ending at the steel
gate with cattle grid at the top of the hill.
Look to the left for a green and yellow
path sign: a black metal gate gives access
to a narrow waymarked path that runs
along the edge of a garden. At the far end,
cross the wall and follow the signs to
climb steeply uphill. The path then
meanders across rough, undulating
moorland, but it is well signposted. After
a few minutes, it starts to run parallel to a

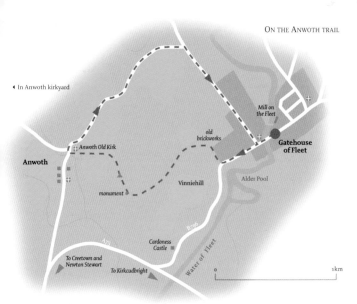

◄ In Anwoth kirkyard

Gatehouse
of Fleet

Mill on
the Fleet

old
brickworks

Anwoth

Anwoth Old Kirk

Alder Pool

Vinniehill

monument

Brig

Cardoness
Castle

Water of Fleet

To Creetown and
Newton Stewart

To Kirkcudbright

0   1km

drystone wall which it accompanies over a small hill. A descent for 50m takes you to a gap in the wall, where you then cross a fence and follow the path through gorse and grassland and up to the monuments.

There are three features on the hill. The first is the needle monument to Reverend Rutherford, the first minister for the parish of Anwoth: he is considered the most famous resident of Anwoth to date and was closely linked with the Covenanter movement in the area. Next, walk to the cairn, erected in 2000 in recognition of the work of the ministers of Anwoth and Girthon, then on to the trig point. From the trig point, head away from the monuments, keeping all three in a line behind you as they disappear from view.

Here, you should find a rough path

which drops down and bends to the right, passing a wooden post waymarked in green and yellow. The path is followed into the woods and downhill to a fence at the lower edge of the woods. Go through the metal gate and cross a boggy field towards a graveyard.

Emerging onto the road, turn right to pass in front of Anwoth Old Kirk, which featured in scenes from the 1973 film *The Wicker Man*. Anwoth is regarded as one of the must-see sites for fans paying homage to the cult classic. Continue along the road past isolated houses and, at the T-junction, turn right to walk back to Gatehouse of Fleet. When this road reaches another T-junction, turn left, crossing the river to reach the start.

Gatehouse to Sandgreen

Distance **12km** Time **2 hours 45**
Terrain **roads and tracks**
Map **OS Landranger 83**
Access **bus (431, 517) from Newton Stewart and Kirkcudbright, (500) from Dumfries and Stranraer**

Pack a picnic and head for the beach via the grounds of the hotel built by the founding family of Gatehouse.

Gatehouse of Fleet is a tranquil village today, but 200 years ago it was at the forefront of the industrialisation of the cotton textile industry in Scotland. By 1790, Gatehouse contained four spinning and weaving mills, a brewery, a tannery, a foundry and a soapworks. By 1825, the river was canalised to create a shipping port and another canal built to help power the industry. However, the industry began to decline because it could not compete with steam-powered factories in Glasgow

and Northern England. The Mill on the Fleet, built in 1788, now enjoys a new lease of life as a visitor centre; you'll also see evidence of the old canalisation of the River Fleet along the road out of town as it passes Cardoness Castle.

Start at the main public car park in Gatehouse of Fleet, opposite the entrance to the Mill on the Fleet. Return to the road and turn right, walking the length of the street to the clocktower, where you turn right onto Ann Street: the large houses at the end were once cotton mills. The road then bends to the right, bringing you to a gap in a high wall. Pass through this and continue straight along the track ahead, with the bowling green to your right and houses and gardens to the left. At a T-junction with a single-track road, turn right and follow it through the woods: this is the driveway to the Cally Palace Hotel.

After meandering across the golf course,

it eventually reaches the front of the hotel. The Cally Palace is a neo-classical house that was originally designed and built between 1759 and 1765, but has had parts added over the centuries, the latest addition being a wing that is not entirely in keeping with the rest of this magnificent building. It was built for the Murrays of Broughton, a local landed family who benefited from the cotton industry that briefly flourished in Gatehouse. Cally Palace is thought to have been the first house in Southern Scotland built of granite ashlar masonry, probably from the Kirkmabreck Quarry.

Pass the front of the hotel, following the tarmac track to the far end of the car park and then into a wooded area: the route is marked with National Route 7 cycle signs. After a further 100m, the track goes under the A75. As it passes Cally Mains Farm, it loses the tarmac but is still a good surface. Further on, the track leads you through a gate, signposted for Sandgreen, and eventually enters a caravan park. Follow the path through the park onto a sandy beach that offers great views west along the Galloway coast. It's a lovely spot for a picnic and a paddle. To return, simply retrace your steps. Except when trees are in full leaf, you'll have views of Cardoness Castle on the return walk: this 15th-century towerhouse is worth a visit (admission fee) as, of course, is the Mill on the Fleet at the start point.

◀ Fleet Bay at sunset

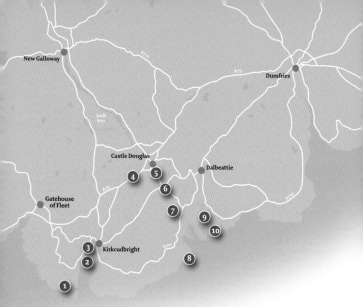

New Galloway

Dumfries

Loch
Ken

Castle Douglas

④ ⑤

Dalbeattie

⑥

⑦

Gatehouse
of Fleet

⑨

⑩

③ Kirkcudbright

②

⑧

①

Roughly bounded by the River Ken/Dee in the west and the edge of the River Urr catchment in the east, the area historically forming the East Stewartry contains three key settlements, each with a distinctive flavour. Kirkcudbright promotes itself as the Artists' Town and has parallels with St Ives in Cornwall for the quality of light that creates an almost magnetic appeal for painters. Once a significant port, the harbour is still busy with leisure craft and the streets a pleasure to stroll through.

Inland, the market town of Castle Douglas is strategically placed on the junction of the A75 and A713, linking east, west, north and south, and has gained a reputation as Dumfries & Galloway's Food Town. Southeast of Castle Douglas,

Dalbeattie was once a major industrial centre, and the remnants of old ammunition factories as well as active granite quarries can be seen around here. It is in a great situation for exploring the nearby forest and the stunning Colvend Coast between Kippford and Southerness.

These towns are set in a predominantly rural landscape, characterised by rolling drumlin scenery and a patchwork of farmland and forestry. Small rocky outcrops create easy hill walks that afford great views for minimal effort, Screel Hill being a fine example. The East Stewartry Coast is a designated National Scenic Area and the entire coastline, with its rich history of fishing and smuggling, is dotted with hidden gems, among them the villages of Kippford and Rockcliffe.

Kirkcudbright, Castle Douglas and the coast

Brighouse Bay circular

Distance 7km **Time** 2 hours
Terrain farm tracks; muddy, sometimes
exposed paths; one fairly steep climb
Map OS Landranger 83
Access no public transport

**A circular route with all that is best about
this part of Scotland – solitude, wildlife
and great views.**

Start at the Brighouse Bay public car
park, signposted from the B727 between
Kirkcudbright and Gatehouse of Fleet.
Walk back up to the road, cross over and
pass through a metal gate onto a path,
which is waymarked throughout.
This leads through a field, where another
gate gives access to a single-track road.

Turn left to climb up along the road,
which passes Ploughmans Cottage after a
few minutes and then enters the yard of
Cairniehill Farm. The route keeps left of

the buildings and exits the farmyard onto
a small track that rises slightly as it passes
between two stone walls.

Around 100m further on, the track
comes to the meeting point of three
gates, where you turn left and accompany
the track as it then swings right and
descends a gentle slope with a wire fence
to the left and drystone wall to the right.
At a junction of fields and gates after
another 100m, follow the waymarks for
Borness Bay along a broad grassy track,
which again runs between a drystone wall
and a wire fence.

This section of the route wanders
through patches of gorse and, after
passing through two gaps in drystone
walls, it arrives at a wooded area with a
bench and information boards. The lower
ground to the right is Cairniehill Loch –
more of a pond than a loch – which forms

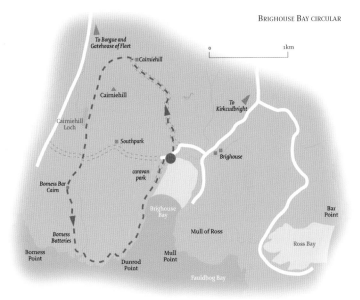

part of a valuable wetland area: details can be found on boards beside the water.

Keeping the wire fence to your left, carry on along the path to pass a track junction and go on through a wooden gate. Beyond a cottage, the route crosses a farm track and continues directly ahead through a metal gate into a field of saplings. In 100m, the path begins to descend towards the sea: look out for a small turning off to the right. This path rises to and crosses a stile, then climbs alongside a wall to reach the summit cairn of Borness Bar, which has a marvellous panorama out to sea and as far as the Isle of Man and Cumbria. Once you have tired of the views, follow the path ahead to drop down towards some

wooden gates and the sea. (For a shortcut, you can descend from the cairn by a path that leads into the caravan site, crossing the site to return to the car park.)

After 100m, the path passes through another gate, then drops down through a gap in a wall to a bench, where you can pause and enjoy a different – but equally impressive – perspective on this stretch of coast. The path now runs along the edge of cliffs on a gradual descent towards the sheltered bathing beach of Brighouse Bay.

Eventually, the path turns into the bay and enters woodland. Go right at a fork to skirt the edge of the Brighouse Bay caravan site. When the path reaches a slipway, continue around to the left and follow the path back to the car park at the start.

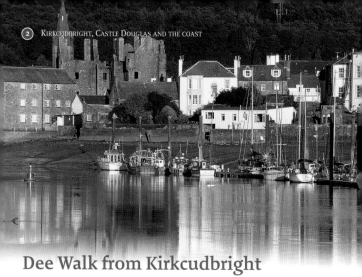

Dee Walk from Kirkcudbright

Distance 7km **Time** 1 hour 45
Terrain pavements and paths; time this
walk with care as the river has a high
tidal range, making the route muddy
and occasionally impassable
Map OS Landranger 83 **Access** bus (505)
from Dumfries, (431, 517) from Newton
Stewart and Gatehouse, (501, 502) from
Dumfries, Dalbeattie and Castle Douglas

**Follow the tidal River Dee north from
Kirkcudbright to pass an Iron Age hill
fort, a hydro-electric power station and
an historic Telford bridge.**

Start at the Harbour Square car park in
Kirkcudbright. Leaving the car park, walk
towards the fishing harbour, then turn
right and take the path towards the
bridge. At the bridge, cross the road and
accompany the footpath on its journey,
signposted Dee Walk, along the river.

After passing local businesses for 1km,
the path leads into a park, exiting at the
far end to reach a wooden footbridge after
200m. Cross this and turn left along the
path as it continues to trace the course of
the river for just under 2km, before
starting to meander back towards the
road. When you eventually reach the A711
into Kirkcudbright, cross it and follow the
path through a gate into fields on the far
side: it is signposted.

Carry on under the remains of what was
a buttress to a redundant railway bridge.
At this point, look up and to the right to
see the distinct outline of an Iron Age hill
fort. The path then reaches a metal gate,
which you go through to accompany the
path for a further 200m through
woodland to a road. Turn left for a
roadside stretch which crosses a bridge
and meanders uphill to a T-junction. Take

◄ Kirkcudbright waterfront

a left here and follow the path past the front of the Tongland Power Station. Built in the 1930s, this is one of a number of generating stations feeding off the Rivers Dee, Ken and Doon. It was built by the Galloway Water Power Company and is a listed building. The power station has a dam which can be clearly seen on the walk: have a look for the salmon ladders built into it. There is a visitor centre open seasonally, which is well worth a visit.

Eventually, you come to the junction of the A711 and A762, with the railway bridge buttresses you passed earlier to your left. Turn left onto the A711 to Kirkcudbright. The road immediately leads across the Tongland Bridge. Built in 1804 with grey sandstone from Arran and red sandstone from Annan, this was one of the earliest large span bridges to be designed by Thomas Telford and the first of his major bridges in Scotland. It was also the first bridge to use weight-saving hollow-ribbed spandrels rather than solid masonry arches. The decorative parapets and castellated towers are thought to have been designed by Alexander Nasmyth.

After crossing the bridge, either retrace the river route or follow the A711 for 1km until it reaches the edge of Kirkcudbright. Around 200m after passing the 30mph sign and town crest, you'll see a low wall and steel grille on the river side of the road. Go through the gap by the steel grille and turn immediately left to cross the wooden bridge and retrace your steps into the harbour square. There are ample opportunities for refreshments in Kirkcudbright.

Map labels:
To Castle Douglas
Tongland
power station
Tongland Bridge
fort
To Gatehouse of Fleet
River Dee
Kirkcudbright Bay
Kirkcudbright Bridge
Kirkcudbright
To Dundrennan

0 — 1km

St Mary's Isle

Distance 6.5km **Time** 1 hour 30
Terrain pavements and muddy paths
Map OS Landranger 83 **Access** bus (505)
from Dumfries, (431, 517) from Newton
Stewart and Gatehouse, (501, 502) from
Dumfries, Dalbeattie and Castle Douglas

**Walk along the shore of the peninsula
that sits between Kirkcudbright Bay and
Manxman's Lake, just 3km south of the
town harbour.**

St Mary's Isle is not an island but a
narrow peninsula which was once the site
of a 12th-century Augustinian priory
dedicated to St Mary. In 1775, St Mary's
Isle was also the location for a minor
event in the American War of
Independence. John Paul Jones, born at
Arbigland, near Dumfries, had moved to
North America where he joined the US
Navy and eventually became the
commander of the US Navy frigate, *Ranger*,
tasked with attacking the Cumbrian and
Solway coastlines. After launching an
attack on Whitehaven, he then sailed into
Kirkcudbright Bay, hoping to capture the
Earl of Selkirk. The Earl, however, was
absent from his home on the isle, so the
men sent to kidnap him demanded
valuables from the Countess instead. She
handed them over and the raiders left the
isle. Years later, the valuables were
returned by Jones with apologies. He later
became known as the 'Father of the Navy'
in the US, but was considered a pirate in
the UK. There is a John Paul Jones Point
on the eastern shore of the isle.

Start at the Harbour Square car park in
Kirkcudbright. Leaving the car park, head
back towards the crossroads, where you
should take a right turn and follow the
road past the Stewartry Museum (open
year round). Some 500m past the
museum, where the road starts to bend

left at the junction with Castledykes Road, you'll see a driveway straight ahead with concrete gateposts and black iron railings. Go through the gates and walk along the tree-lined avenue.

After a few hundred metres, the tarmac stops and the drive continues as a gravel and dirt track to pass through woods. Just after a track joins from the left, the path swerves right, with an open field to the left encircled by iron railings. Continue along the track until it swings left up a gentle incline, where you leave it for a footpath on the right. This skirts the shoreline, where the remains of an old boathouse and a slipway can be seen along the way. It carries on around the tip of the peninsula where, depending on the season and tree cover, the Little Ross Island Lighthouse can be seen. This was the site of a famous murder. In 1960, two lighthouse keepers were on the island when one was murdered and the other went on the run. The alarm was raised when a local resident, who was out sailing, decided to stop for a chat with the lighthouse keepers and discovered the body. The murderer was eventually caught in Yorkshire and sentenced to death. No explanation has ever been given for the crime.

Eventually, the path starts back towards Kirkcudbright. At a T-junction, turn right onto a track to keep to the shoreline.

Continue straight ahead along the path when a track joins from the left, now passing a field with iron fencing to the left. Once beyond the fence, the path reaches another T-junction, where you turn left and, at the next T-junction after 50m, turn right. This rejoins the original track: simply retrace your steps to the start. There is plenty to extend your stay in Kirkcudbright for, including the National Trust for Scotland's Broughton House and Garden on the High Street (fee), the ruins of the 16th-century Maclellan's Castle (fee), the Tolbooth Arts Centre or simply a pleasant stroll around the streets.

Threave and the island castle

Distance **12.5km** Time **3 hours 45**
Terrain **muddy paths, roads and farm
tracks** Map **OS Landranger 84**
Access **bus (500) from Stranraer, Newton
Stewart and Dumfries, (503) from
Dumfries, (501) from Kirkcudbright,
(520) from Ayr**

**An atmospheric walk from Castle
Douglas to view Threave Castle, followed
by a stroll around the 1500-acre estate
with an optional detour to the famous
gardens at Threave House.**

Start at the public car park between the
library and the tourist information centre
in Castle Douglas. Leave the car park at
the end nearest the tourist information
and turn left onto King Street. Continue
to the crossroads at the clocktower,
turning right here to walk for 50m to
another crossroads. Take a left turn onto
Cotton Street (note, Church of St John the

Evangelist on the far right corner). At the
end of this street is a T-junction, where
you turn right onto Blackpark Road to
pass the Threave Rovers football ground
and the wastewater treatment site.
Continue as the road becomes a track and
rises over a small bridge. About 100m
beyond the rise, where the track swerves
right, turn left off the track through a
metal gate, signposted Threave Estate,
and follow the path out of town.

This path takes you under the A75 in
500m, reaches a wooded area and goes
through a metal gate, before passing
under a bridge 200m further on. From
here, climb the steps to the right and
accompany the track for 100m to a car
park. At the car park, follow the signs to
the castle. Another 1km along well-
maintained paths brings you to a ferry
that crosses the River Dee: this is the only
castle in Scotland located on an island in

a river. To summon the ferry, simply ring the bell located by the jetty. A trip to this 14th-century tower is always memorable, but please note this is an Historic Scotland site and is subject to an entrance fee and seasonal opening.

To continue the walk, or miss out the castle (cutting around 1 hour and 3km from the walk), carry on past the bridge for another 800m until the path meets a road. Take a left turn onto the road and follow it as it passes over the A75, then go immediately through a wooden gate off to the left to walk through a Scots pine wood and then over open farmland. Cross a footbridge and then a road to take the rising path into more woods. The path then descends to another footbridge and meets a single-track road, where you turn left with views of the castle. Where the road passes a house called Hightae after 500m, turn left to pass the house and access a footpath via a wooden gate. (Alternatively, to tour Threave House and gardens, turn right through a gap in the stone wall. Owned by the National Trust for Scotland, this fine Scottish baronial

house is open to the public, but Threave is perhaps better known for its 64-acre sloping ornamental garden, whose many highlights include the glasshouses, the children's discovery garden, a secret garden and a visitor centre with restaurant and shop. Both the house and gardens are subject to an entrance fee and seasonal opening.)

Beyond the wooden gate, the footpath continues through a series of gates before emerging between two houses. Follow the road past the houses and look out for some steps on the right that lead up to another path. The route then takes you across a road, along a farm track and over a bridge that crosses the A75, where a wooden gate opposite gives access to the path. At a path junction after 150m, turn right for Castle Douglas to return under the A75 and into town.

◂ Threave Castle across the water

Carlingwark Loch from Castle Douglas

Distance **6.5km** Time **1 hour 45**
Terrain **good footpaths, boardwalk**
Map **OS Landranger 84** Access **bus (500)
from Stranraer, Newton Stewart and
Dumfries, (503) from Dumfries, (501)
from Kirkcudbright, (520) from Ayr**

**Take the Lovers' Walk around the tranquil
loch on the edge of Castle Douglas for
good views and plenty of wildlife.**

Castle Douglas has been settled for
centuries, though, at 200 years old, its
contemporary name is relatively new.
It developed in the 1600s as a staging post
for armies being sent to Ireland by James
I/VI because of its location on a major
military road. It has always been known
as an important stop on routes that
eventually became the A75. It also
developed as a centre for cotton spinning,

but could not compete with larger
manufacturing centres such as New
Lanark. The current town is arranged
around three parallel streets – King,
Queen and Cotton Streets.

Start at the public car park between the
library and the tourist information centre.
Leave the car park at the end nearest the
tourist information, and turn left onto the
High Street. Walk along this street to the
crossroads with a clocktower on the
corner, where you take a left onto
St Andrew's Street and follow this road
across Queen Street and past St Ninian's
Church. The loch soon becomes visible on
your right and then the pavement runs
alongside it.

At the far end, go through a wooden
gate to follow the path along the edge of
the loch, noting the green and yellow

Dumfries & Galloway footpath sign.
As you continue, look out for a path
detouring to the right which leads to
a bird hide. The loch is well known as
a nesting site for many species of birds,
including mute swans, tufted duck,
shoveler and great crested grebe.

After passing through a number of
gates, the path goes through a wooden
gate to reach a T-junction. Turn right
onto boardwalk which, after 100m,
becomes a grassy path. The boardwalk
crosses marshland and allows good
views, especially to your left where
Bengairn and Screel Hill dominate
the skyline. The marshland is a
designated Site of Special
Scientific Interest (SSSI) for its
botanical and wildlife interest.

When the path meets the road
at a T-junction, turn right to
accompany the road as it passes a
cluster of houses and then bends
up and to the right. Although this is a
quiet road, it pays to take care as there
is no footpath or pavement. The church
near the houses is Kelton Church: the
graveyard contains the mausoleum of the
Douglas family, whose home was the
nearby Gelston Castle. Further along the
road is the entrance to Threave House:
follow the road as it bends right away
from this and eventually meets the B736
at a T-junction. Turn right here to return
towards the town centre, with the loch
now to your right, continuing along the

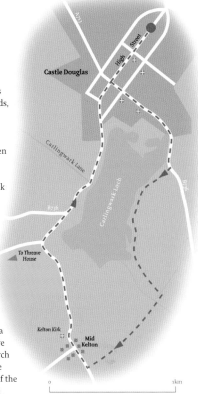

road as it leaves the water and becomes
the High Street. Simply walk uphill along
this street to the car park. As you would
expect of Dumfries & Galloway's official
Food Town, there are ample opportunities
for refreshments in Castle Douglas.

Gelston Castle

Distance 3km **Time** 1 hour
Terrain paved roads and muddy tracks;
buggy-friendly if using alternative start
Map OS Landranger 84 **Access** bus (516)
from Castle Douglas

**Enjoy the peace and quiet on this walk
around the once grand estate of the
family that gave the town of Castle
Douglas its name.**

Start the walk from the crossroads in
the village of Gelston, which lies 5km
south of Castle Douglas along the B727.
Look for a footpath sign opposite the war
memorial and follow this into the woods,
where a path leads you in a pleasant
meander through the trees. Around 250m
from the start point, the woodland path
meets a vehicle track, which you turn left
onto. (To reach the same point with a
buggy, you can walk along the road for

around 50m, turning left onto the track at
a pink gatehouse.) Route finding is made
easy by the provision of arrow posts along
the walk.

After 500m, the track reaches a building
with a courtyard and a tower. This was
once the stable block to the estate, but
has been converted into holiday cottages
and business premises. Follow the track,
now tarmac, as it goes around the stable
block, where the remains of the 'castle' are
visible through the trees to the left. This
was the home of Sir William Douglas, the
founder of Castle Douglas. Built around
1805, this Adam-style red sandstone
country house took the form of a hugely
oversized toy fort.

After curving around the former stable
block and past a walled garden, the
tarmac track crosses a small bridge over a
walled burn. Just past the bridge, the track

◀ On the way to Gelston Castle

forms a Y-junction: take the right fork to
carry on the walk (signposted) or the left
to detour down the main driveway to the
gatehouse and back: it gives a feel for the
sweeping approach that visitors would
have enjoyed as they arrived at the house
many years ago.

Back to the main route after the fork,
continue to curve right on a slight incline,
heading into woods and past a timber
yard and stables. This track eventually
reaches a gatehouse, the South Lodge,

where you turn right onto the road and
walk back to the crossroads and the start.

On the return section along the road,
there are some great views back across
the estate to the former stable buildings.
Up to the left, you can see Dunguile Hill
Fort on the horizon and a motte closer to
the road, identifiable by their stepped
profiles. Simply continue along the road
to the start. The nearest refreshments are
in Castle Douglas.

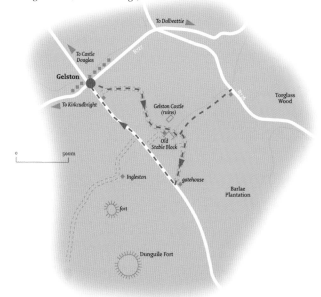

Screel Hill scramble

Distance 6km Time **2 hours 30**
Terrain **forest tracks, boggy paths; steep
in places, easy scrambling**
Map **OS Landranger 84**
Access **no public transport**

**An entertaining hill walk with good
waymarking, easy scrambling and
brilliant views.**

This route gives a fantastic introduction
to hillwalking, with some limited
exposure and a bit of scrambling on the
ascent. The views are great and make the
summit plateau feel far higher than its
modest 350m. In places, the walk is well
marked by green posts; however, it still
requires some navigation on the summit
plateau if visibility is poor. As it can get
muddy, walking boots are recommended.

Start at the Forestry Commission car
park, located 500m along a single-track
road just off the A711: the turning is 2km
north of Auchencairn and 3km south of
Palnackie. A forestry track leaves the car
park past a metal gate to meander
through the trees for around 500m. The
track eventually reaches the entrance to
an open field on the left. At this point, go
through a gap in a stone wall, noting the
green post with red and yellow markings,
to join an upward-trending footpath.

After 300m, the path reaches a forest
track and a wooden bench, where you can
pause to enjoy the views and contemplate
the rest of the climb. Cross the forest
track to accompany the footpath as it
plunges into thick forest and weaves
uphill through the trees, with green
wooden posts with yellow markings
showing the way. In another 300m, the

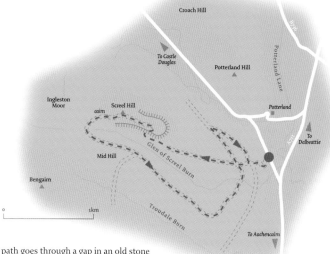

path goes through a gap in an old stone wall and the woodland becomes less dense, so the climb ahead can be seen a bit more clearly. After a further 200m, the path comes into a clearing where a bench is well located for you to take a breather and absorb more views.

Continue along the path as it ascends past a rocky outcrop to the right, giving good views to the left. Another 200m and the path takes a sharp turn to the right on a rocky ascent to the summit plateau. Take care as this can feel exposed in places and a bit of scrambling may be needed towards the top. Eventually the path reaches a wide plateau where, depending on the weather, the summit cairn may be visible only 800m away. A clear but boggy route crosses undulating ground to the summit

cairn, with great views across the surrounding countryside: on a good day Criffel, the Lake District, Bengairn, the Galloway Hills and the Lowther Hills can all be seen.

To leave the summit, continue along the path as it drops down a steep slope. At the bottom, the path enters dense forest, with a drystone wall to the right. Eventually, you take an obvious path off to the left that initially goes uphill, then drops through thick woodland until it reaches a forestry track. This is followed on a meandering journey down the hillside to reach the bench met on the earlier ascent. Carry on along the forest track for the remaining gentle descent to the car park.

◀ Screel Hill from Potterland Farm

Smugglers' coast from Balcary

Distance **7.5km** Time **2 hours**
Terrain **muddy, often overgrown paths
(wear long trousers), exposed in places**
Map **OS Landranger 84**
Access **no public transport**

**A walk across windswept clifftops and
through farmland in an area rich in
smuggling history.**

Start at the public car park adjacent to
the Balcary Bay Hotel. This is found down
a minor road and signposted from the
A711 at Auchencairn, the pretty village
just over halfway from Kirkcudbright to
Dalbeattie. The area around Auchencairn
is dotted with small mines, which were
created to extract barytes, a naturally
occurring pink-hued mineral used in the
manufacture of a range of products from
televisions and cars to paints. Perhaps
better known is Auchencairn's

associations with a thriving smuggling
trade. In the 1700s, the Solway was famous
for smuggling, with many caves in this
area used for storing contraband such as
tea, whisky and lace. It is said that the
Balcary Bay Hotel was set up as a front for
smuggling from the Isle of Man, with
passageways and cellars underneath that
were used to hide the contraband. The
area's smuggling fame was captured by
Sir Walter Scott in his novel *Guy Mannering*,
chiefly located in Galloway, and by S R
Crockett in *The Raiders*, whose fictional
location was based on Hestan Island in
Auchencairn Bay.

From the car park, walk to the end of the
road and turn onto a muddy path,
signposted Balcary Point and Rascarrel.
This leads to a gate into a field, again
signposted for Balcary Point. Here, you
can either take a faint path around the left

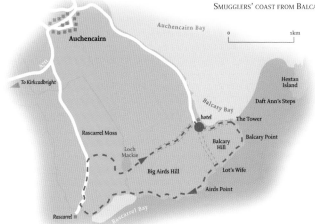

Auchencairn Bay

0   1km

Auchencairn

To Kirkcudbright

Hestan
Island

Daft Ann's Steps

Balcary Bay

hotel   The Tower

Rascarrel Moss   Balcary Point

Loch   Balcary
Mackie   Hill

Big Airds Hill   Lot's Wife

Airds Point

Rascarrel   Rascarrel Bay

side of the field or follow the telegraph poles: both take you to a metal gate giving access to woodland. The path begins to climb as it makes its way through the trees, before emerging through a metal gate onto open, gorse-clad moorland.

As the path follows the cliff edge closely, it does feel exposed and a head for heights is required, but the views east along the coast and towards Cumbria more than compensate. This is also a good stretch of coast for birdwatching and you are likely to find yourself in the company of seabirds such as guillemots, cormorants, fulmars and razorbills. The path begins a gentle descent, passing through a metal gate bizarrely placed across the route. (For a shortcut to the start, simply follow the path off to the right.) Beyond the gate, the path becomes less exposed as it drops to the shoreline and picks its way west.

Beyond some timber huts, a vehicle track takes you along the coast before turning inland to reach a metal vehicle gate. Follow the track out of a car park, keeping the river to your left. When this meets a single-track road, turn right onto the road and follow it uphill. At a layby, where you'll see an old wooden signpost to Balcary, turn right onto a muddy path into the woods. After a few metres, the path opens onto an old tarmac forestry track, which you accompany for 200m before turning right onto a dirt path along the edge of a Scots pine plantation. This path then crosses a wooden footbridge and skirts the edge of Loch Mackie. After passing through a metal gate, you continue alongside fields, past a farmhouse and downhill to the car park. This last descent gives excellent views of the coast and Criffel. Refreshments can be found at the hotel or in Auchencairn.

◀ Looking towards Screel Hill

71

Kippford to Rockcliffe Riviera

Distance 4km **Time** 1 hour 30
Terrain roads, muddy tracks and paths
Map OS Landranger 84 **Access** bus (371, 372) from Dumfries and Dalbeattie

A circular coastal walk between two pretty villages, taking in an ancient hill fort and some great views along the way.

Start from the main car park in Kippford, around 5km south of Dalbeattie. From the car park, continue along the road to a junction, where you follow the road left as it climbs, passing houses and giving an elevated view of the estuary: this is the start of the Jubilee Path. Eventually, a footpath bears right into woodland managed by the National Trust for Scotland. Follow this well-maintained path as it leads through wooded areas interspersed with gorse and bracken to emerge at a junction with a gate into a forestry area called Markhill. The area around Kippford is criss-crossed with paths, many of them signposted and equally well maintained. The Markhill path is 3km in length and offers an additional expedition if wanted. At the Markhill junction, take the path on the right, signposted Mote of Mark, to go through a gate and wood, before heading through another gate and following the path to the left.

After 25m, at a path junction, turn right for a steep but short-lived climb up a path and stone steps, which lead to the top of the Mote of Mark, an ancient hill fort with commanding views of the Rough Firth and the Solway. A sweep of the coastline takes in Screel Hill, Bengairn, the Solway, the Cumbrian coast and the halfway point

on this route – the village of Rockcliffe.

Returning down the path, turn right at the track junction, go through a gate and cross the meadow to a wooden enclosure near a burn. Inside the enclosure is an information board with details on the history of the Mote of Mark: this is a good opportunity to pause and take a look at the location of the old hill fort.

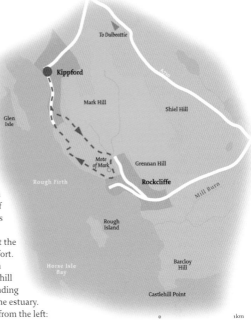

From the information board, while facing the hill fort, follow the track leading left downhill towards the estuary. After 30m, a path joins from the left: this runs from the village of Rockcliffe itself. To detour into the village, turn left here, cross a wooden footbridge and follow the path through a meadow and a metal gate to turn left again. The village fringes a small bay and is a great place to rest for a while or get refreshments.

To bypass the village, follow the track as it curves to the right with the water's edge immediately to your left. Cross a cattle grid and then accompany the track as it rises and curves right. After a few metres, by a stone painted with a white arrow and

'Kippford', a path leads off to the right. Follow this into the trees and on a wandering course under powerlines to eventually reach a Y-junction. Take the left-hand option to drop downhill, passing between houses and meeting a road at the water's edge. Turn right here for a roadside walk through the houses to the start point. The route passes some interesting artwork along the way, with welcome refreshments available in Kippford.

◀ Rockcliffe seafront

Sandyhills to Rockcliffe

Distance **7km** Time **2 hours**
Map **OS Landranger 84** Terrain **road,
tracks and muddy, undulating coastal
paths** Access **buses (371, 372) from
Dumfries and Dalbeattie to Sandyhills
also stop in Rockcliffe for the return**

**A magnificent walk along clifftops,
around quiet bays and through secluded
villages with spectacular views at every
turn. This route can be walked in reverse
or as an extension to the previous walk
from Kippford.**

Start from the car park in Sandyhills
beside the public toilets and near the
holiday park entrance. From the car park, a
boardwalk path leads to the beach, where
you turn right and follow the signposted
path around the back of the bay. After
crossing a wooden footbridge, keep to the
path straight ahead as it rises to a flat
grassy area. Go over this area to ascend
the steps (signposted) to a metal gate
and into a field. At the far end of the field,
pass through another gate and climb to
the summit of The Torrs. A topographic
point board helpfully illustrates the view
across the Solway.

After soaking up the views, begin the
gentle descent – still on the path –
towards the village of Portling. On the
way, the path crosses a number of stone
walls via steps, joining a tarmac track once
it reaches the village. Accompany the
track uphill, then turn left at the white
road sign. The road climbs, then drops
towards the sea with Port O'Warren Bay in
the distance. Eventually, you'll see the
white footpath sign, where you turn right
to cross another wall and ascend once
again on a path.

In a while, the gradient starts to ease
and the path meets a stone wall. Cross
this and, at the far end of the field, go over

◄ Hestan Island

a wooden stile. This section gives excellent views towards the Rough Firth, Balcary Bay, Hestan Island and Rockcliffe; off to the right are the hills of Bengairn and Screel. The path then steeply descends through a field, crosses a stone wall (a stile is placed 50m uphill if needed) and hops over a number of boggy burns (most with stepping stones), before coming to another wooden stile. Beyond this, the path runs along the edge of some cliffs, marking the start of a briefly exposed section. It then drops to a ruined farm building with a secluded sandy bay to the left.

Continue along the path as it climbs, then descends again with the destination of the day now in your sights. The path swings left to Castlehill Point, so called as it was the site of an Iron Age fort; a topographic point board is provided at the summit. From Castlehill Point, follow the path downhill, through a metal gate and along the edge of the field, keeping with it as it veers left into the trees for a meander, leading through a metal gate and past the grave of a sailor called Nelson – not *the* Nelson. The path then runs along the back of a beach, through trees, across another beach and between more trees to emerge at a T-junction with a tarmac track. Turn left onto the track and follow it past houses to meet the main road in Rockcliffe.

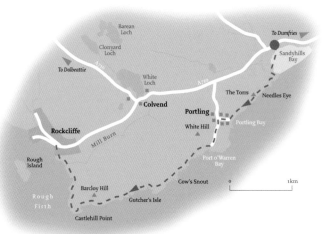

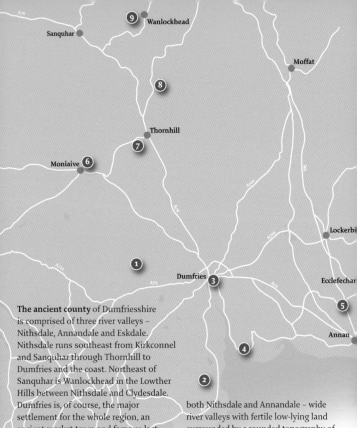

The ancient county of Dumfriesshire is comprised of three river valleys – Nithsdale, Annandale and Eskdale. Nithsdale runs southeast from Kirkconnel and Sanquhar through Thornhill to Dumfries and the coast. Northeast of Sanquhar is Wanlockhead in the Lowther Hills between Nithsdale and Clydesdale. Dumfries is, of course, the major settlement for the whole region, an ancient market town and famous last home of Robert Burns.

Annandale extends from Moffat in the north to the red sandstone town of Annan on the Solway, and was historically a thoroughfare for both friendly and hostile visitors. It has strong links with Robert the Bruce, and was given to the family by David I in 1124. The landscape of both Nithsdale and Annandale – wide river valleys with fertile low-lying land surrounded by a rounded topography of hills – has more in common with the Borders to the east or Cumbria to the south than with Galloway, As you move further into Annandale, there are strong cultural links with the Borders too: for this reason the routes in this chapter focus primarily on Nithsdale, with just one route venturing from near Annan.

New Abbey in winter ▶

Around Dumfries and Nithsdale

Glenkiln sculpture trail

Distance 8.5km Time 2 hours
Terrain **paved road, suitable for buggies, and rough path, which isn't**
Map **OS Landranger 84**
Access **no public transport**

Take a culturally rewarding stroll that passes artworks set in imaginative locations along a delightfully quiet valley west of Dumfries.

Although Glenkiln Reservoir makes a pleasant walk in its own right, it is the sculptures scattered across the open landscape that make this an atmospheric and unusual visitor attraction. They have taken up residence here thanks to the passion of the landowner Sir William Keswick, who started collecting the artworks in 1951 and sited the pieces – not without some controversy – in imaginative locations across his land.

Start this walk from the car park at the north end of the Glenkiln Reservoir. This is located off the A75, around 11km west of Dumfries near the village of Shawhead, from where it is signposted. As a linear route, this can be walked on tarmac so is suitable for buggy access, and can also be completed on bike or horseback.

Park in the public car park, where your cultural journey begins immediately with the first sculpture, *John the Baptist*, by Auguste Rodin which looks down on the car park and its occupants. Rodin (1840-1917) is considered the pre-eminent French sculptor of his time, most famous for his works *The Thinker* and *The Kiss*. The sculpture in Glenkiln was made in 1878 and said to have been modelled on an Italian peasant: although both feet are firmly planted on the ground, the figure somehow appears to be walking.

Leave the car park and turn right to continue north, crossing the cattle grid to

◀ Sculpture in the trees

walk to the Cornlee Bridge and view *Standing Figure* by the celebrated sculptor and artist Henry Moore (1898-1986). Born in Castleford, Yorkshire, Moore is best known for his monumental bronze abstract figures, of which this is a good example. He was an official war artist during WWII and went on to make many pieces for public display, with a substantial part of his earnings going into the Henry Moore Foundation.

Retrace your steps and continue beyond the car park for around 700m, keeping an eye on the high ground to the right for Moore's *Glenkiln Cross* and, a bit further on, the *King and Queen*. For a closer view, you can go through the gate directly below and cross the fields to reach either of the pieces.

Carry on along the road for a further 1km until a road joins from the right: take this road and, after 500m, you will see another work by Moore. This is *Two Piece Reclining Figure No 1*, an abstract sculpture that is placed on a hillock to the left of the road.

To find the final sculpture, continue along the road for a

further 700m to meet a track (not suitable for buggies) leading off to the right through a gate. Along this track is *Visitation* by Sir Jacob Epstein (1880-1959). Epstein was born in New York, but moved to London in 1905 and became a UK citizen. He worked extensively in bronze and was well known for portrait and monument sculpture. *Visitation* is a bronze cast of the Virgin Mary in a scene from the bible.

From this sculpture, simply carry on along the track until it meets the road at the *King and Queen*. Turn left to return to the car park.

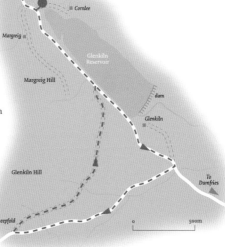

To Dunscore

Cornlee Bridge

Cornlee

Margreig

Glenkiln Reservoir

Margreig Hill

dam

Glenkiln

Glenkiln Hill

To Dumfries

sheepfold

0   500m

Conquering Criffel

Distance 5km **Time** 2 hours
Terrain tracks and worn paths over peat
bog; this is a hill walk and conditions can
change fast, so take a map, compass and
waterproofs **Map** OS Landranger 84
Access bus (371, 372) from Dumfries and
Dalbeattie to New Abbey, 4km from start;
or follow the A710 south from the A75 at
Dumfries, turn off the A710 to the
car park near Ardwell Farm (GR971634)

**A short but strenuous walk that rewards
the effort with views across the Solway to
the Lake District. With straightforward
navigation, Criffel is a great introduction
to hillwalking in the area.**

From the car park, cross the farm track
and go through the gate which is clearly
signposted. Take the next right onto a

pathway between two drystone walls. This
leads uphill into woodland: as it ascends
through the trees, look out for the
striations, or grooves, created by glacial
abrasion on the exposed rock of the path.
The trail continues to rise and runs
alongside Craigrockall Burn, crossing
two forestry tracks and eventually
reaching the fence that marks the edge of
the woodland. After crossing the second
forestry track, the path meanders across
the burn via wooden bridges. This section
can get very muddy and slippery in places,
so after heavy rain, it makes sense to
ignore the bridges and stay on the left-
hand side of the burn all the way to the
boundary fence.

Once through the fence, follow the path
left as it climbs towards the summit: this

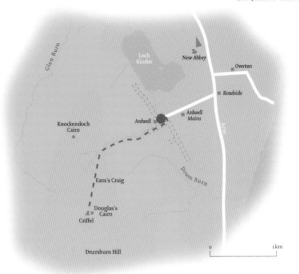

stage crosses open moorland and offers good views towards Dumfries and across the Nith Estuary. The body of water below is Loch Kindar, which supplies the water for the mill in New Abbey through a 1km-long lade that ends in a pond near the mill. Three islands are visible in the loch: the largest is home to an old kirk while the smaller two are crannogs (man-made islands) dating from pre-Roman times.

The nearest village beyond the loch is New Abbey: it is worth a visit for refreshments, to see the mill in operation and to visit Sweetheart Abbey, which is visible from the summit. The abbey was founded in 1273 by Lady Devorgilla de Balliol in memory of her late husband John Balliol, the founder of Balliol College, Oxford. As further testament to her devotion, Lady Devorgilla carried her late husband's embalmed heart in an ivory casket until her own death some 20 years later, when it was buried with her at the abbey. The monument above New Abbey is the Waterloo Monument, built in memory of the soldiers who defeated Napoleon in the battle of June 1815. Above this looms the peak of Knockendoch, which can be incorporated into this walk to make a longer day out. Although the latter stage across moorland can be hard going, the summit, consisting of a cairn and trig point, is soon reached. Enjoy the views and then simply retrace your steps.

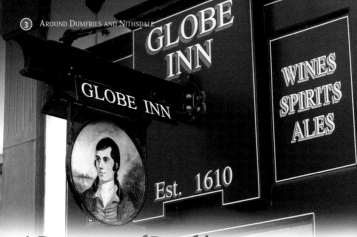

A Burns tour of Dumfries

Distance 2km **Time** 30 mins (but add time
for the museum and visitor centre)
Terrain buggy-friendly pavement
Map OS Landranger 84 **Access** regular buses
and trains from Glasgow and Carlisle

**Follow in the footsteps of the great bard
and uncover some of Dumfries' vibrant
history along the way.**

Start at the Whitesands car park and bus
stance. Alternatively, to begin the walk
from the railway station, exit the station
on either side and walk up to the road
that crosses the bridge over the station.
Turn right and follow this road – at first
named St Mary's Street and later English
Street – into the town centre.

Facing the river, bear right towards the
pedestrian Devorguilla Bridge, the oldest
multi-arch stone bridge in Scotland. At
the far end is a small museum which is
well worth a visit for the detailed history

of the bridge and origins of Dumfries
that it provides.

Turn left after crossing the bridge and
follow the path along the riverside to the
attractive Robert Burns Centre, also worth
visiting for its free exhibition. Continue
along the river to the pedestrian
suspension bridge and cross back over
the water. On the other side, turn right
and then take a left onto St Michael's
Bridge Road: this leads to the statue of
Jean Armour, Burns' wife. Worth a detour
is St Michael's Kirkyard, located across the
road. It is the church where Burns and his
family worshipped and the cemetery is
where Burns is buried.

Back at the statue, turn left onto
Burns Street and follow it to the
museum, located in the house in which
the bard lived between May 1793 and his
death in July 1796. The building has been
a place of pilgrimage for enthusiasts

◀ The Globe Inn

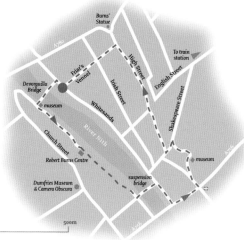

throughout the centuries, with Coleridge, Wordsworth and Keats among the many eminent visitors.

Carry on along Burns Street until it reaches a T-junction with Shakespeare Street. Turn left here, then immediately right onto the High Street. A walk down this street leads you past the Globe Inn Close, which retains much of the atmosphere that made it Burns' favourite drinking den. Further along the High Street, you pass the Dumfries Mid Steeple, built in 1703 as a new building for use as council offices, prison and armoury. It was constructed using local red sandstone and timber from woods near Newton Stewart. On the side is an iron panel showing mileages to various towns in the UK, including one to Huntingdon. This seemingly random choice of English town highlights the importance of farming to this area, because it was the destination for drovers moving cattle to markets for sale and consumption in London. In the 1820s, between 20,000 and 30,000 head of cattle were traded in this way every year. The Mid Steeple was also where Burns' body lay in state after his death in July 1796. Just past here is the Queensberry

Square, where Burns would have paraded during his time with the Dumfries Volunteers militia in 1795.

Also on the High Street, look out for the Hole in the Wa' Close with a pub at the end, another of the bard's favourite haunts. The High Street eventually meets Church Street, a good place to stop and appreciate the scale of the Burns statue, built in 1882 and paid for by public subscription: its size and location indicate the importance that the poet has always held for the town. After this, turn left and follow the narrow Friar's Vennel downhill towards the riverbank and the start. There are plenty of places to stop for refreshments in Dumfries, and you can easily make a longer day out by calling in at the museums and visitor centres passed on this walk.

Exploring Caerlaverock

Distance **3.5km** Time **1 hour**
Terrain **muddy tracks and paths**
Map **OS Landranger 84**
Access **no public transport**

Explore the saltmarshes and mudflats of an important national nature reserve before visiting Caerlaverock Castle.

Start from the car park on the B725, 4km south of the village of Glencaple. Walk through the metal gate at the far end of the car park and follow the well-marked all-ability path into woodland. After around 100m, you reach a Y-junction, which marks the end of the all-ability trail. The main route branches left into Castle Wood, a semi-natural woodland known to have been in existence since 1750: it is home to native tree species such

as oak, hazel, birch, holly, ash and alder. If you have time, first make the detour along the right-hand path, which runs for 50m to the edge of the merse, or saltmarsh, part of the wetland nature reserve that supports huge numbers of wildfowl and wading birds. The merse is often grazed by cattle and sheep, which controls the growth of grasses, and is especially important for barnacle geese: the entire population migrates to the Solway from Svalbard in Arctic Norway and a large proportion winter at Caerlaverock. It is a key site for curlew, oystercatchers and shelduck, as well as being the most northerly outpost for the rare natterjack toad.

Returning to the main route, follow the path as it crosses a burn via a wooden

◀ Caerlaverock Castle

bridge and reaches a stand of spruce trees. Off to the right is a detour to a very stylish bird hide: the estuary in front of you is Blackshaw Bank, a mudflat which is home to the shellfish and worms that feed the many types of waders and wildfowl found around here. Rejoin the path and carry on along a clear route interspersed with boardwalks and small bridges. The trail crosses an expanse of water by a bridge, then passes some houses and continues along a muddy vehicle track. This eventually reaches the edge of the Caerlaverock Castle grounds, marked with a Historic Scotland board. At this point, look right for a small nature trail through the woods: this rejoins the track a bit further along.

Here, you can either retrace your steps or enter the Historic Scotland grounds: there is a fee. The first castle visible at this point consists of little more than foundations: it was abandoned around 1277 due to subsidence into the wetlands. The next castle is the fantastic Version Two, built on slightly better ground out of red sandstone and still standing proudly today. The castle has a unique triangular layout with a double-towered gate and a water-filled moat. Its location so close to the English border has also guaranteed a lively history. In the grounds, you can see a replica trebuchet, used in sieges for throwing stones and other missiles. Returning the same way, you get good views across the estuary towards Criffel, Knockendoch and the Waterloo Monument near New Abbey.

For a full day out, you can drive further along the road to the Wetland Centre (fee), with its coffee shop and bookshop, picnic area, observation towers, hides and seasonal nature trails.

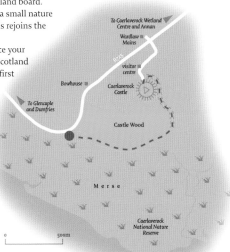

Hoddom and Repentance Tower

Distance 4km Time 1 hour 20
Terrain roads and dirt tracks
Map OS Landranger 85
Access no public transport

Follow the peaceful River Annan to a stately lookout post that offers great views in all directions.

Start this walk from the car park and picnic site on the junction of the B723 and B725, 6km northwest of Annan. The walk can be completed in either direction or started from the caravan site. Leave the car park to follow the blue and white arrow signpost into woods on a path laid with boardwalk in places. When this eventually meets a single-track tarmac road, cross the road and note the signs to turn left onto the riverbank path. After 200m, at a junction, follow the right-hand track to carry on along the river. (Dog owners should take the left option to the front of the castle and pick up the walk there, as the right-hand route passes through the golf course, a dog-free zone.)

Accompany the track as it skirts the golf course. At a fence, cross the stile and amble along the riverside to a footbridge. Don't cross; instead follow the signs to turn left and cross the field in the direction of Hoddom Castle. The path then enters woodland: go through a gate, turn immediately left and cross a small bridge, keeping to the path and signs as you meander through the woods.

Hoddom Castle was built in 1568 by John Maxwell as a main residence in the West March. It was defaced during the Victorian era with ill thought-out extensions to the top of the tower and its

86

◀ Repentance Tower

surroundings. The castle is a remnant of the Border Wars between England and Scotland that took place between the 13th century and the crowning of James I/VI in 1603. When the path reaches the side of the castle, turn left and walk around the front – the far end of the castle is where dog walkers rejoin the route – to climb uphill along the road, keeping the children's play area to the left. Depending on the season, refreshments are available in the castle.

The route is now in what must be one of the best caravan sites in Scotland: where else can the camper wake up and have breakfast in a castle? At the far end of the play area, take the campsite road off to the right, signposted for Repentance Tower. At a second signpost, turn off the campsite track and cross a small patch of grass to a third signpost pointing through some woodland. After approximately 100m, the woodland path meets a road, where you turn left for just 100m of road walking, before turning off at the wooden steps to the right. The tower is a short slog across a field.

Once you have gained the tower, you will enjoy the panoramic views. To the south are the Lakes and Solway, to the west is Criffel, to the north are the

Lowther Hills and a great view down to Hoddom Castle, and finally to the east can be seen the M74 and the Border hills in the distance. This tower was built for signalling and as a lookout for the castle occupants wary of invading armies and cattle thieves in the surrounding area. It is thought to have been called Repentance because it was built on the remains of a chapel. When you tire of the views, return to the road and then turn right to accompany it back to the car park.

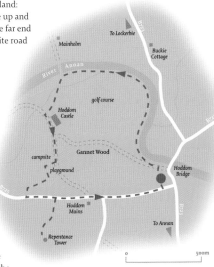

Moniaive and Bardennoch Hill

Distance 7.5km Time 2 hours
Terrain roads, grassy and dirt tracks;
gentle ascent Map OS Landranger 78
Access bus (202, 212) from Thornhill, (202)
from Dumfries

**From the charming village of Moniaive,
explore forest, moorland and quiet
country lanes on a gentle hill walk.**

Moniaive has existed since the 10th
century, its name deriving from the Gaelic
*monadh-abh*for, 'Hill of streams', and
referring to its situation at the head of
three glens – the Craigdarroch, Dalwhat
and Castlefairn. In 1636, Charles I granted
Moniaive a 'free burgh of barony' which
enabled it to set up a market and prosper.

The village has strong artistic links and
was the home of James Paterson, one of
the founder members of the Glasgow
Boys, who lived in the village for 22 years.
More modern art connections can be
found on a challenging walk to *Striding
Arches* – red sandstone sculptures dotted
round the head of Dalwhat Glen, around
10km west of the village.

Start the walk from the free public car
park in Moniaive. Leave this and turn right
to walk through the centre of Moniaive.
At the house with the clocktower – the
former schoolmaster's house – turn right
and follow this road past a low stone wall
to reach a track, signposted for
Bardennoch, to the right.

Take this track across a bridge and up
the hill. Where this eventually reaches a
junction, take the waymarked left-hand
trail that carries on up the hill. After

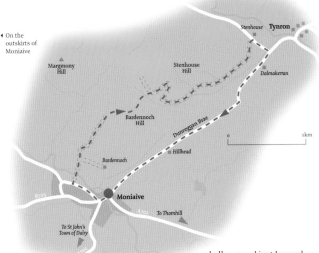

◀ On the outskirts of Moniaive

passing a wood on the right, the track enters a field by a metal gate and continues to rise. It then runs between two drystone walls in varying states of decay, goes through three more gates and passes a ruined farmhouse.

Once beyond the farmhouse, follow the track uphill as it skirts a small Scots pine plantation, keeping the trees to the right as you make your way to the summit of Bardennoch Hill: there is a faint path for guidance. After enjoying the views, maintain the same course to drop down towards the trees below. On the descent, keep the wall marking the forest boundary to the right and look out for a metal gate that leads into the trees: note a

shallow pond just beyond.

Once into the forest, turn right on the track to walk parallel to a field boundary wall, soon leaving this wall for a steep descent, followed by a downhill straight to the forest edge.

The track finally leaves the forest and passes through a number of fields separated by farm gates. A last gate leads onto a single-track road, where you turn right and right again at the next T-junction.

This road climbs steeply uphill with hazelwoods either side. After around 2km of climbing, the road reaches its highest point and begins to drop down into Moniaive. The descent offers fine views of the village as it unfolds before you, and runs all the way back to the car park.

1939
THE CENTENARY OF
THE BICYCLE
THE NATIONAL COMMITTEE ON CYCLING
HONOURS THE MEMORY OF
KIRKPATRICK MACMILLAN
THE INVENTOR OF THE BICYCLE
He builded better than he knew

Penpont and Keir Mill

Distance 5.5km **Time** 1 hour 30
Terrain roads and muddy tracks
Map OS Landranger 78 **Access** bus (202, 215) from Dumfries and Thornhill, (212) from Moniaive and Thornhill

A gentle riverside walk taking in two quiet villages and the unassuming birthplace of the bicycle.

Start from the public car park in the village of Penpont, 5km west of Thornhill. From here, walk back to the crossroads and continue over it to follow the road as it meanders out of the village. After crossing a roadbridge, immediately turn onto the waymarked riverside pathway. This is the Scar Water, which drains into the Nith around 2km south of Keir Mill. The river is a haven for wildlife, and it is possible to watch goosanders and heron

feeding here. The riverside is lined with ash, alder and oaks, but in winter the waters can clearly be viewed through the bare trees. Benches are located at intervals if you wish to stop to contemplate the scene. The path can be muddy along this section.

Eventually, the trail wanders away from the river, passes beneath some houses and ascends the bank to reach a small bridge over a burn. Once over the bridge, the path meets some steps and climbs up to the road. Turn right for an on-road stretch into the hamlet of Keir Mill. On entering the settlement, look out for a signpost to the grave of Kirkpatrick Macmillan (1812-1878), commemorating the man popularly credited with inventing the pedal bicycle. To find his grave, skirt the fence of a large house by

◀ Memorial to Macmillan

a muddy path to the walled cemetery; the gravestone is at the far end.

Return to the road and turn left into the centre of Keir Mill. At the-T junction, bear right to walk on the wide, quiet road that takes a straight line back to Penpont, with good views of the wide valley each side. After 500m, you'll see a lone white house on the left: this is the smithy where Macmillan lived and worked. A plaque on the wall details how he was responsible for developing the pedal cycle. Around 1824, he started working for his father, the local blacksmith, and noticed a passer-by riding a 'hobby horse' bicycle (propelled by the riders putting their feet on the ground). He decided he could improve the design by engineering pedals on the front wheel which drove the back wheel via connecting rods. He was often seen riding his bicycle to Dumfries and as far afield as Glasgow, a journey of more than 100km. He never patented the design and others quickly realised the potential. With this in mind, a plaque was displayed at the smithy with the apt phrase: 'he builded better than he knew'.

The road heads back into Penpont, joining the outward route. Refreshments are available in Penpont and 6km west in Moniaive, which has pubs and an organic teahouse. There are more options in Thornhill, including the excellent Thomas Tosh café, art gallery, gift and bookshop in the old parish hall.

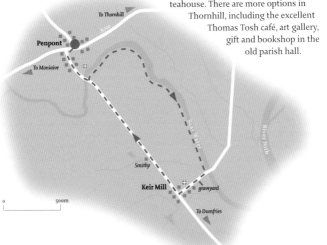

Durisdeer Well Path

Distance **6.5km** Time **1 hour 45**
Terrain **muddy tracks, boggy sections**
Map **OS Landranger 78**
Access **no public transport**

An atmospheric walk along the isolated valley of the Kirk Burn which visits the site of a well-preserved Roman fortlet.

Durisdeer is a tiny and relatively little-visited village located 10km north of Thornhill at the foot of the Lowther Hills. It was once on a main thoroughfare for the Romans who passed right through the village. The outward leg of this walk follows the Roman road.

Start from the village square and take the dead-end road that runs along the right-hand side of the churchyard. After passing a number of houses, go through the gate at the end and follow the track running along the glen. After around 1km, a fingerpost points off the track to the Roman fortlet. Go through the gate and

proceed to a ford over the burn (using the stepping stones), through another gate and along the track to the fortlet. On the approach, the fortlet seems to rise out of the ground: it's worth taking time to walk around what is considered one of the best preserved of its kind in Britain. It is 31.5m by 18m in size, and an entrance can be found across a faint ramp. It is thought to be from the 1st century AD and was sited to guard the Well Path, the Roman road linking the valleys of Nithsdale and Annandale.

At this point, a choice can be made either to retrace your steps for a shorter walk of 3km or to continue up the valley for the full circuit. For the longer route, carry on up the glen on the muddy track to reach a tin shed. From the shed, aim for the corner of the drystone wall ahead. On the way to the wall, the track becomes indistinct and is crossed by numerous burns which create boggy patches, so pick

◄ The Lowther Hills

out your route with care. Once at the wall, simply follow it uphill to the saddle: the old outlines of the Roman road become more visible along this part of the route.

Once the gradient eases, look out for a metal gate in the wall and pass through it to walk the short distance to a farm gate across the track: it is worth having a closer look at the gateposts, which appear to be old distance posts from this track, the Old Edinburgh Road. The road developed for pilgrims to Whithorn from Edinburgh, passing through Penpont, Dalry and Minnigaff/Newton Stewart. It fell into disuse when the Dalveen Pass, 3km north of Durisdeer, opened in the 18th century to become the main route between Nithsdale and Annandale.

From the gate, take the obvious track back down the glen to the start. Towards the top of the valley are good views towards the Galloway Hills off to the west. Further along is an excellent outlook over the Roman fortlet, which gives a feel for the part it would have played in local life.

Back at the start, pay a visit to the

lovely churchyard. This is larger than would be expected for such a small village due to the fact that it contains the burial vault of the 1st and 2nd Dukes of Queensberry, the family whose home is the nearby Drumlanrig Estate. Also found here are the gravestones of Daniel McMichael, an executed Covenanter, and William Lukup, the master of works at Drumlanrig. The 'pink palace' of Drumlanrig Castle, located some 7km southwest of Durisdeer, is also worth a visit: there is a fee for accessing the house, gardens and walking/cycle trails.

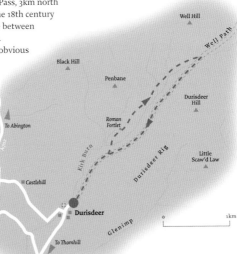

Wanlockhead treasures

Distance 7.5km **Time** 2 hours
Terrain roads and tracks; some ascent
Map OS Landranger 78 **Access** bus
(221) from Sanquhar, (224) from Dumfries

A strenuous hill walk which starts from Scotland's highest village and rewards with magnificent views.

Start from the Museum of Lead Mining in Wanlockhead, a high and lonely moorland village which can, however, be exceptionally pretty when the weather is fine. At the far end of the museum car park, go up some steps, cross a small grassy area and a road, then follow the track past some newer housing on the left. This stage is well signposted with Southern Upland Way (SUW) markers. Once beyond the houses, the track crosses open heather moorland and the rounded domes ahead are filled with various

aerials, masts and a 'golf ball' (the radar at the top of Lowther Hill). Where a track peels off left, carry straight on, keeping the golf ball dead ahead to join a tarmac road. Turn right and follow the road uphill and around a sharp left bend where, at the end of the crash barrier, you turn onto the crosscountry path with its SUW waymarkers.

The path eventually rejoins the road, where you turn right to climb along it. At a left bend, look out for a gap on the right, between sets of crash barriers. Go through this gap to walk across country for around 100m to a track with a wire fence: turn right onto this to descend to a saddle, marked by a wooden gate and electricity pylons. Ascend the hill on the other side of the saddle, keeping the wire fence to your left. Eventually, the gradient eases as you approach the summit of East

94

◀ Welcome to Wanlockhead

Mount Lowther (also known as Auchenlone). The locator post at the top is showing signs of age, though the indicated points are still visible and, since it was erected in 1944, it's not in bad shape!

With good visibility, the top of Auchenlone is ample reward for the effort. It is possible to see Goat Fell on Arran, the Paps of Jura, Ben Lomond and Ben More, the Lowther Hills and Hart Fell; to the south can be seen the upper fells of the Lake District, including Scafell Pike, and some of the landmarks of the Solway coast and Galloway Forest, including Criffel, Cairnsmore of Fleet, the Merrick, Corserine and Cairnsmore of Carsphairn.

After enjoying the views, return to the saddle and follow the path to the left that runs beneath the electricity pylons. Keep to the path as the pylons veer away downhil, eventually crossing a burn and rejoining the tarmac road at a bend. Retrace your earlier steps to the start.

Refreshments are available in Wanlockhead at the highest pub in Scotland and at the museum (fee for visiting the exhibition; seasonal opening). Wanlockhead has developed since Roman times as a mining and smelting centre for lead, gold and silver. Between the middle ages and the early 20th century, the area was the centre of Scottish lead and precious metals mining. The village still has many features of the old industry, including mine shafts, pumping engines and spoil heaps: it is worth taking some time to follow the visitor trail. Wanlockhead also hosts the British gold-panning championships and, should you wish to try your luck in the rivers around these hills, equipment and lessons are available from the museum.

Index